THE WORDS OF MY TESTIMONY

THE WORDS OF MY TESTIMONY

A Life Saved from Darkness-The Way, The Truth and The Life

LIZZY RAMASODI

"And they overcame him by the blood of the Lamb, and by the word of their testimony, and they loved not their lives unto the death"

REVELATION 12:11.

It has been a privilege and an honor to write this book. It was started and finished by the grace of God. May the Lord bless you and manifest his power in your life as you read this book, in the mighty name of Jesus Christ.

TABLE OF CONTENTS

INTRODUCTION

The Book of Revelation 12:11 says, "And they overcame him by the blood of the Lamb, and by the word of their testimony, and they loved not their lives unto the death." This statement is very true based on personal experiences. The blood of Jesus Christ, the blood of the lamb of God has saved my life and the lives of many who have chosen to trust the word of God and put their trust in the name of Jesus Christ and what he did at Calvary. The blood of Jesus Christ cleanses us from all unrighteousness and gives us a testimony of victory over the gates of hell and the enemy. I recall one night in a dream/vision state, the enemy said to me, "How sure are you that you will enter heaven?" and I said, "I will enter because of the blood of Jesus," and the enemy disappeared immediately.

The blood of Jesus Christ is so potent that it literally nullifies all the accusations the enemy lays upon believers in their everyday lives. The blood of Jesus moves people from darkness to light; from deception of the enemy about life and lifestyles, to truth and freedom; from sin, transgressions and iniquities to forgiveness; from hopelessness to hopefulness; from weaknesses to strength; from unrighteousness to righteousness; from defeat to victory; from hell to heaven, from death to life. It is the blood of Jesus Christ that breaks all curses in people's lives and gives those who choose Jesus Christ blessings that only God can give. It is the blood of Jesus that protects those who believe in Jesus Christ and defends them from spiritual and human enemies. It is the blood of Jesus Christ that translates people from the torments of generational curses to the pleasures of generational blessings.

In this book, I would love to share the word of my testimony, my life's journey to Jesus Christ as candid as I can possibly share without implicating anyone.

Everyone is born in a fallen world characterized by sin. Everyone is a sinner the minute they enter this earth and take their first breath. Newborn babies have not sinned by themselves; they, by default, inherit the sins of those who came before them. As children become toddlers, they begin to speak, and the nature of sin begins to manifest without anyone teaching them to sin. It is because when Adam and Eve sinned against God, humans lost their inherent holiness because sin separated humans from God.

As we traverse through the journey of life, we meet many people who impact us in different ways and make impressions, some positive and some not so positive, in our lives, especially on our inward parts, our mind, heart, soul and spirit. These are the parts that are unseen to the naked human eye and cannot be touched by human hands, and their impact is expressed through our words, actions and experiences. It is at this level that sin resides. The blood of Jesus Christ penetrates the heart, mind, soul and spirit to cleanse people from sin.

The first people most human beings encounter when they enter earth are family members in the household they are born into, close relatives and family friends. A child comes to trust these people and look up to them as they form their perspectives of life. These groups of people can have lasting impressions with dynamics and dimensions that can last a lifetime in a life of person, through their actions and words. The grooming and upbringing a person receives are complemented by family practices and beliefs that are passed from generation to generation in the family, and have the power to shape the individual's character and influence their values, perspectives, experiences and outcomes in life. This is because the impact of that exposure is at a spiritual level. This, in turn, is acted out at the physical level. The foundational beliefs and practices of the family of birth are generally the origin of generational curses and/or generational blessings.

LIFE IS SPIRITUAL

LIFE AND THE FOUNDATIONS A PERSON STANDS ON

From the moment of birth, every human connection and engagement is meaningful in its own way and within its own right. No human ever really remains the same after most connections they make. Some connections are short-lived with an altering impact, while others are long-lasting with consequences that last a lifetime. Everyone at every stage is impacted to some degree by the connections and engagements they encounter in various setups, whether in person or online. The impact could be minor or life-transforming, even long after the encounter.

Human encounters are spiritual. I have come to believe that every human connection, for whatever purpose, be it pleasant or unpleasant, serves a divine purpose. That divine purpose is spirit-led and can lead a person into their God given destiny or divert them from their God given destiny.

Life is spiritually governed by spiritual laws. The spiritual makeup of a person tends to attract certain life experiences and people into their life, aligned with their spiritual purposes. As a result, each person is here on earth to fulfill a divine purpose, whether people are conscious or ignorant of it or not. It is each person's responsibility to discover that divine purpose. The divine purpose can be inspired by the Holy Spirit or by evil spirits. The divine purpose can be for good or evil.

Life is in dichotomy. Where there is good there is also evil and bad, where there is light there is also darkness and the same goes for right and wrong, holy and unholy, Jesus and Satan, Holy Spirit and evil spirits, God and idols and false deities, boy and girl, married and single, clean and dirty, win and lose, righteous and unrighteous, faith and fear, love and hate, the gospel and doctrines of demons, salvation and sin, grace and captivity, mercy and cruelty, freedom and oppression, bondage and deliverance, sickness (physical, spiritual, economic, social) and health, life and death, godly and ungodly, the list is endless. The dichotomy of life reflects the two (2) kingdoms ruling in the lives of people on earth.

The path of life to our destination is not always straight, clear and direct. The dichotomy of life cannot be avoided because of the spiritual nature of life. The dichotomy makes life a spiritual warfare. Every day, humans are fighting to overcome the powers that oppose them or to hold on to the powers that support them. What makes the difference is whether a person submits to Jesus Christ and the kingdom of God or Satan and the kingdom of darkness. Depending on who the person submits to, they are victorious or defeated in this life and in the life after death.

Every human being submits to a spirit. As we know, God is a spirit and Satan is a spirit too. In John 4:24, it says, "God is a Spirit, and those who worship him must worship him in spirit." As Satan is also a spirit, those who worship him worship in spirit and falsehood. The thing about Satan is that he likes people to think that he does not exist and that there is no hell. He wants people to think of their experiences as just life and not spiritual. On the other side, God wants everyone to know about him, that he exists and is accessible through the path he gave to those who believe.

God wants people to get saved and come and be with him in heaven. The whole process of salvation is purely spiritual. What happens to a person and in the spirit when one gets saved cannot be explained with human knowledge and cannot be seen with the naked eye, but the evidence is a changed life in the physical.

Human beings need a savior. No one can save themselves and be good enough to get into heaven because everyone is born in sin through Adam and Eve, who committed the original sin of disobedience to God. This original sin recycles itself and is exacerbated by societal and family

12

beliefs and practices that keep people away from God. This is the reason Jesus Christ came to save people from themselves. Jesus came as a human being, in the flesh, to reveal God to people. He revealed himself to those he had created and showed the way to heaven, cleansed people from sin through forgiveness by his blood and gave the Holy Spirit to those who believed and put their trust in him and the gospel.

The spirit works through the human being. The spirit needs a human body to express itself. Every human action is governed by a spirit. When God created humans, he breathed the spirit of life into them so they could become alive. However, through the original sin, other spirits found a pathway to inhabit the human vessel. When Adam and Eve sinned, the Holy Spirit left them as the spirit of sin entered them and held them captive to its desires. The difference is that God is the spirit of freedom, and Satan is a spirit of bondage. The Bible says, "Now, the Lord is that, Spirit; and where the Spirit of the Lord is, there is liberty, 2 Corinthians 3:17. Jesus Christ came in the flesh to express God who is Spirit, to set humans free from the original sin and the captivity of Satan, and equip his children to proclaim to the lost world the good news of the gospel. On the other hand, Satan has his children who are filled with contrary spirit from the Holy Spirit, who promote life away from God via various social, economic, spiritual, legislative and other means and include everyone who does not believe in Jesus Christ and the gospel. Life of affliction is an inheritance for those who are without Christ.

The good thing about God is that through Jesus Christ, who is God, the hope to overcome the afflictions of the devil came into the world. Jesus Christ has revealed the power of God to set captives free. Even the Bible in Psalm 34:19 says, "Many are the afflictions of the righteous, but the LORD delivers him from them all." The righteous children of God never suffer indefinitely. God delivers them from the multitude of afflictions.

However, the afflictions of the unrighteous are endless because, without God, the enemy of humans who possess and control their souls is free to afflict and have his way. Jesus Christ is the only power to deter the enemy, who is Satan, demons, evil spirits and his agents. Those who are without Jesus Christ are always in compromised positions. Whatever solution they receive, it is temporary. That is why they go into different spiritual paths of religious practices, traditions, and spiritual rituals to deal with their afflictions or resort to a lifestyle of carnality. In turn, they become slaves to those practices, traditions, rituals and lifestyles because the devil is not interested in setting anyone free. He is a task master with no compassion for his slaves.

Those with Christ Jesus need only to pray in His name and can be set free and overcome all evil. Life is spiritual. Another beautiful thing about God is that he gives those who believe in Jesus Christ and in his name the power to become the children of God (John 1:12) and nullify the spiritual inheritance from Adam and Eve. In the name of Jesus Christ, they have the power to crash the dragon, the head of the ancient serpent, the enemy and his works as well as deliver and heal other people. This is because those who believe in Jesus Christ become born again, not of blood, nor of the will of the flesh, nor of the will of man, but of God (John 1:13). It is the most supernatural experience anyone can ever receive.

As we journey to achieve our purposes and destinies, there are many distractions in reaching God given destinies and purposes. The good thing is that there are also opportunities to define and redefine, position and reposition, refine and restore to minimize or eliminate those interruptions. The longer you live, the more distractions and opportunities you get. The extent and the depths of distractions and opportunities depend in many ways on the person's position in the spiritual realm, which determines the material world. Every person living has a spiritual position from the day they are born. At birth, everyone has the same spiritual position as Adam and Eve, and the spiritual status is inherited from their family of origin, just as people inherit material possessions. This spiritual makeup lasts until a person gets born again of the Spirit of God. This means that a person can change their spiritual makeup and status as they grow by giving their life to Jesus Christ. If they don't, they feed their original status by maintaining the spiritual practices, beliefs and rituals of their families or choose another path that keeps or increases the intensity of their original spiritual makeup. Any practice that is without Jesus Christ is with the devil. Any spiritual practice, belief and ritual that is without Jesus Christ is witchcraft, it does not matter how it looks on the outside or whether it involves prayer to a god of any name.

By the spiritual, I refer to the world that one cannot see with their own naked eyes. When we pray, we do not see with our naked eye what happens, but there is a lot that happens. What we see is the answer we receive, which came from spiritual activities that were triggered by prayer. The same goes for the words we speak and the thoughts we entertain. Hebrews 11:3 (NKJV) says, "By faith we understand that the worlds were framed by the word of God, so that the things which are seen were not made by the things which are visible."

It is important to remember that the Word of God is Jesus Christ. As stated in John 1:1-5, 9, 10, 14 (KJV), it says, "In the beginning was the Word, and the Word was with God, and the Word was God. The same was in the beginning with God. All things were made by him, and without him was not anything made that was made. In him was life, and the life was the light of men. And the light shineth in darkness, and darkness comprehended it not. That was the true Light which gives light to every man coming into the world. He was in the world, and the world was made by him, and the world knew him not. And the Word was made flesh and dwelt among us, full of grace and truth. People beheld the glory of Jesus Christ, which we still behold to this day, as of the only begotten of the Father."

The Bible also expounds on this notion that life is spiritual, saying the things we do not see are eternal and the things we see are temporal, urging us to look at the things which are not seen to understand the things we see. In 2 Corinthians 4:18 (NKJV), it says, "While we do not look at the things which are seen, but at the things which are not seen. For the things which are seen are temporary, but the things which are not seen are eternal."

It is important to note that the spiritual realm controls the physical realm. Therefore, there needs to be an alignment between the spiritual and material realms in a person's life to realize one's divine purpose and destiny. Divine purpose can be of God or of the devil. The divine purpose of the devil can be clear and straightforward, such as criminals, assassins, witches, human traffickers, kidnappers, etc. and sometimes masquerading as God, such as false deity(ies) found in the religions of the world that are without Jesus Christ as their Lord and Savior or as lifestyle practices like yoga. Not everything that looks divine is sponsored by the Spirit of God, the Holy Spirit. The devil and his demons and evil spirits can sponsor anything that is without Christ that looks divine and clean, masquerading as blessings and a good life.

Whatever happens in the spirit realm during dreams or waking hours, as well as the spiritual status of a person, determines their blessings, curses and experiences in the material world. Everything starts in the spiritual realm before it manifests in the physical realm. Even in the Bible, God says in the book of Jeremiah 1:5, "Before I formed you in the womb I knew you; before you were born, I sanctified you, I ordained you a prophet to the nations." This indicates that what prophet Jeremiah became in the material world was made of what happened in the spirit realm that was not seen with the naked eye. Truly, Jeremiah became in the physical material world, that which God called him to be before he was even formed and born. The call was made in the spirit realm and manifested at the appointed time in the physical material world.

The enemy can do the same. Once a person conceives a child, demonic powers can tamper with the child's development, blessings and destiny from the womb. The enemy cannot do this before a person is conceived, as he is not God. Only God can proclaim a person's destiny before they are born. God gives everyone a good destiny. But the devil, using the generational and family sins, transgressions and iniquities to afflict and accuse parents and unborn child, can interfere with the purposes of God for that child and family. Also, the enemy can program curses and afflictions to manifest in a person's life and family at a given time, and sometimes it can take years before the manifestation.

If you are to be blessed, that blessing will manifest first in the spirit before it becomes evident in a person's life. If there is a curse in someone else's life or a family, such as recurring and persistent troubles and afflictions in a person's life or family manifesting as sicknesses, poverty even if people work and earn good money, no marriage or persistent and recurring single parenthood in the family, premature or common nature of death in the family, accidents, child development issues, divorces, failures, drugs and sexual abuses, immorality and many other things, it first finds expression in the spiritual realm before it manifests in the physical. Successful victory over such curses can only be realized through the name and the blood of Jesus Christ.

COVENANTS AND ALTARS

Covenants and altars play a huge role in the transactions between the spiritual and the material world. Covenants can be done while people are awake or in their dreams when they are sleeping for as long as there is an altar they are associated with knowingly or unknowingly. Altars are launching pads for covenants. Altars are a place where the spirit meets the physical, where sacrifices are offered, covenants are forged and destinies exchanged. Behind every altar, there is a spirit.

Without an altar, a covenant cannot be enacted. Jesus Christ demonstrated this very perfectly. The cross on which he was crucified has become a permanent altar on earth for those who call on his name. The blood which he shed at the altar of Calvary was a sacrifice that has established a permanent, everlasting covenant on earth to all those who confess with their mouth and believe in their heart that he is the Lord and Savior, the Son of God who came in the flesh. The confession made at the altar of Calvary invokes the blood covenant that in turn changes the destiny of people and families in the spirit and in the physical realm. With this confession and belief, the blood of Jesus then washes away all their sins, iniquities and transgressions and delivers them from generational curses.

When people engage in spiritual practices, the places they use can become altars, or the humans themselves who are immersed in spiritual practices can become altars. An altar can be holy or evil. Places of worship are altars, just like a psychic office or a shrine of a saint, or any other agent of Satan can be an altar. At the altar, covenants are established. It is the covenants established at the altars that give spirits the right to access people in their physical and dream states. Covenants at altars are maintained through sacrifices of all kinds, with the blood sacrifice being the most potent and ultimate sacrifice.

The cross and the blood of Jesus Christ give the Holy Spirit access to believers and interact with them in the material and spiritual realms in a holy way. The opposite is true for those who submit to evil altars. The demons and evil spirits interact with those people in a demonic way and forge evil covenants with them in the waking or dream state. These evil covenants in the dream state cause a lot of harm in the lives of people. The covenant blood of Jesus Christ, established by the cross of Jesus Christ, allows the Holy Spirit to access the spirit man of the person who is born-again. The covenant of the cross is entered into when a person confesses with their mouth and believes in their heart that Jesus Christ is their Lord and Savior.

The blood of Jesus Christ is above all the blood sacrifices that can ever be offered at an altar and is new every day, while the blood of anything, human or animal can never be a permanent sacrifice. That kind of sacrifice needs renewal to keep their altars and the covenants active. This is because God himself, who created all things, through Jesus Christ, shed his blood on the ground and the earth received it as a permanent sacrifice. God redeemed the earth and its inhabitants through his own blood and his blood speaks day and night for those who are born-again.

When a person does yoga, transcendental meditation, visits a shrine or a place of worship that does not worship Jesus Christ, consults with a spirit medium, performs ancestral worship, visits the graves to perform rituals, etc., they also enter into a covenant with the altar and the spirit and deity of that place. These kinds of altars are generally called evil altars. The covenants of these altars then release the spirits of that altar to start interacting with that person. Since people typically engage a lot with altars when they are not with Jesus Christ, all the spirits of those altars will have access to them when they are awake or sleeping to possess and influence them to accomplish their evil deeds and plans. This also applies to families, tribes, nations and continents. The evil spirits from evil altars can never do anything out of character, they only know how to do evil, deceive, kill, steal and destroy.

Depending on the altar the family has submitted to from generation to generation and continues to submit to, the lives of the family members will be influenced by the covenants and spirits of those altars accordingly. It is very dangerous to engage altars that are not of the cross of Jesus Christ. The altar of the cross of Jesus Christ is the only Holy altar on earth, under the earth and in the heavens. It is the only altar that is above all the other altars. The same goes for the covenant blood of Jesus Christ. Other altars are ruled by evil spirits hungry for evil covenants that give them access to family lineages, generation after generation.

For as long as an altar is standing, covenants can be forged. Altars speak and are generally maintained through the blood. Without the spilling of the blood, an altar is as good as nothing. This is indicated in Leviticus 17:11 (NKJV) that says, "For the life of the flesh is in the blood, and I have given it to you upon the altar to make atonements for your souls; for it is the blood that makes atonement for the soul."

Again, in Leviticus 16:5-16 (NKJV), it tells how the blood must be spilled and sprinkled 7 times to atone for sin, uncleanness and rebellion. When Jesus Christ died, he spilled and sprinkled blood in 7 places to deliver humanity from evil altars and atone for sin, uncleanness and rebellion. The altar of the cross of Jesus Christ and his blood spilled and sprinkled speak for born-again Christians before God in heaven and also on earth in their day -to – day living.

Any altar established without God and the cross of Jesus Christ is an illegal and an evil altar. It is an altar of chickens and goats. Some evil altars are maintained through human blood sacrifices, such as during accidents, abortions, or when people cut themselves to spill blood and some through the blood of animals, immoral lifestyle, drunkenness, crime, and many other abominable acts or whatever form the devil prescribes to his children . It is extremely dangerous to enter the spirit realms through an evil altar. Some people have been trapped in the spirit realms while others died because of accessing the spirit realms through evil altars. Addictions are mostly a spiritual trap that keeps addicts in bondage to the evil spirit that feeds from acts of addiction. Addictions are spiritual. The same is also true for most mental issues. The addicts and mental people can be human altars themselves. These kinds of spiritual issues can only be dealt with effectively through the altar of Jesus Christ and his blood. Any physical treatment would yield only temporary results. This is the reason such issues run in a family or a nation.

All evil altars can only be destroyed by the name and the blood of Jesus Christ and the fire of the Holy Spirit to stop them from speaking. Once the altar is destroyed, the covenants are nullified, and the spirits of those altars lose power.

Sometimes it is important to take altars to the court of heaven using the relevant scriptures to present the case before God for their destruction. The reason is that when Jesus Christ died, he entered the Most Holy Place, the Holy of Holies, through his blood on our behalf, and his blood talks for us before God. The animal bloodshed and sprinkling with the law was just a shadow of things to come. The law was to help humans be aware of sin in their lives, teach people how to deal with sin and many other things at an altar with a sacrifice so people would know they need the savior through whom their sins must be forgiven and lives delivered. The altars and sacrifices of the old were to prepare humans that when the final sacrifice comes with Jesus Christ, people would receive it and be delivered without the need for the blood of animals.

It says in Romans 9: 11-15 (NKJV), "But Christ came as a High Priest of the good things to come, with the greater and more perfect tabernacles not made with hands, that is, not of this creation; Not by the blood of goats and calves, but by his own blood, he entered the Most Holy Place once and for all, having obtained eternal redemption. For if the blood of bulls and of goats and the ashes of a heifer sprinkling the unclean, sanctifies for the purifying of the flesh, how much more shall the blood of Christ, who through the eternal Spirit offered himself without spot to God, cleanse your conscience from dead works to serve the living God? And for this reason, he is the mediator of the new covenant, by means of death, for the redemption of the transgressions under the first covenant, that those who are called may receive the promise of the eternal inheritance."

So, when we approach God boldly at the throne of grace in his royal court, it is the blood of Jesus Christ that gives us access to God. It says in Hebrews 4:14-16 (NKJV), "Seeing then that we have a great High Priest who has passed through (ascended) the heavens, Jesus the Son of God, let's hold fast our confession (faith we profess). For we do not have a High Priest who cannot sympathize with our weaknesses, but was in all points tempted as we are, yet without sin. Let us therefore come boldly to the throne of grace, that we may obtain mercy and find grace to help in time of need."

The altar of the cross of Jesus Christ is maintained by the blood Jesus Christ shed when he went to Calvary. The blood of Jesus Christ never loses power. That is the reason Christians do not offer any blood, but rather take the Holy Communion to remember what Jesus Christ has done and renew the covenant. Jesus Christ urged his disciples to take the Holy Communion as often as they can. The Holy Communion renews the covenant of salvation achieved through the death, the burial, the resurrection and the ascension of Jesus Christ into heaven, the Holy of Holies, as often as Christians partake of the holy ceremony.

SPIRITUAL NATURE OF DREAMS

Dreams are not just random things a person sees or does when sleeping. They are deep spiritual manifestations a person experiences while still living here on earth. They are revelations of things to come, whether good or evil or things that happened in the past that need to be taken care of. It is important to recall and remember dreams. Dreams are an effective vehicle to expose the altars and covenants operating in the life of a person. Dreams are in the spiritual realm because the human spirit never sleeps. It is always awake and experiences first that which will manifest in a person later in the physical and material world as an experience of life.

Covenants in the spirit can be forged during the dream state. Both God and the devil can access people during the dream state to forge covenants and/or give a message. God told Joseph in a dream to take Jesus Christ to Egypt because Herod was going to kill children aged 2 and under. Going to Egypt, Joseph agreed to the covenant forged in the dream. As written in Mathhew 2:13 "And when they were departed (the Magi), behold, the angel of the Lord appeared to Joseph in a dream, saying, Arise, and take the young child and his mother, and flee to Egypt, and stay there until I bring you word, for Herod will seek the young child to destroy Him." It is important to note that the act of Herod killing the young children was already done in the spirit before the children were killed in the physical, material world. Herod and Pharaoh, who killed the children in Egypt to prevent the deliverer of the children of Israel from future captivity, had the same spirit. They both were possessed by the spirit of Satan, who was working overtime to ensure the deliverance of the children of Israel from slavery did not happen because through them would come the messiah to deliver humanity from the slavery of sin and the works of the devil. However, with God's providence, we can still evade the experiences we encounter in dreams.

Because dreams are so important, that is the reason the realm of darkness does most of its wickedness in the night when people are sleeping. They await people to go to sleep and attack in their sleep while in their dream state. Whatever gets done there, in the place not seen with the naked eye, becomes what the person sees in the material world eventually. It is by God's sovereign mercy that most people are shielded from the experiences emanating from the dream manipulations of darkness.

Sometimes, it takes a long time before people see the results of their dreams or experience their dreams in real life. The human spirit, depending on what feeds it during the waking state, cooperates accordingly in the dream state. If fed with the things of God, the human spirit will reject and fight anything evil and darkness in the dream state and stop it from becoming a reality in the physical, material world. It is important to remember to pray about the dreams to nullify evil covenants forged in the dream state and stop evil seen or done in the dream from manifesting the plans of the enemy against a person.

It is also important to pray and accept that which was good and came from God in the dream. The Bible says in James 1:17 that "every good gift and every perfect gift is from above, comes down from the Father of Lights, with whom there is no variation or shadow of turning. These gifts can also be given in a dream state.

At times, a person may be born again and feed their soul, spirit, heart and mind with godly food during the waking state, yet the covenants and altars operating in their lineage could make them weak to resist evil attacks in their dreams. The main thing is to remember that there is no condemnation for those who are in Christ (Romans 8:1). When the person wakes up, those dreams and covenants forged in the dream state should be rejected and cancelled spiritually in the name and in the blood of Jesus Christ. The blood of Jesus Christ redeems and cleanses (Hebrews 9:11-15, ESV), and the name of Jesus Christ is above all powers, principalities, dominion and might.

Ephesians 1:19-21 (NKJV) says, "And what is the exceeding greatness of his power toward us who believe, according to the working of his mighty power which he worked in Christ when he raised him from the dead and seated him at his right hand in the heavenly places, far above all principality, and power, and might and dominion, and every name that is named (invoked), not only in this age but also in that which is to come." In Philippians 2:9-10 (NKJV), it says, "Therefore God also has highly exalted him and given him the name which is above every name, that at the name of Jesus every knee should bow, of those in heaven, and of those on earth, and of those under the earth, and that every tongue should confess that Jesus Christ is Lord, to the glory of God the Father."

It is at the mention of the name of Jesus Christ against those evil dreams that they dissipate and never manifest in real life. If one does not pray against them, they do come to pass. I have seen this firsthand. I dreamed of people, and what I saw in dreams about them came to pass; some, I saw their death in the dream. Before I was a Christian, I didn't know that after a dream, we ought to pray to stop the plans of the enemy. The thing is, even if a person prays and they are not born again, their prayer would likely be pointless because it is only at the mention of the name of Jesus Christ that things can truly be resolved. Some people in darkness might do their rituals to address issues and reverse dreams; however, whatever they do pales in comparison to a prayer of a true believer who lives by faith. Even in real life, only born-again Christians have records of raising the dead and many real, lasting miracles performed in the name of Jesus Christ, without any ritual or magic.

No Satan, witches, wizards, fallen angels and demons can resist the blood and the name of Jesus Christ. It's above them all. As the Bible says, every knee shall bow, of things in heaven, and things in earth, and things under the earth, and every tongue confess that Jesus Christ is Lord, to the glory of God the Father (Philippians 2:9-11 (KJV)). This confession is not limited by time and distance, or awake and when in a dream state. Just calling on the name of Jesus Christ anytime and anywhere is enough to send the enemy flying. I have witnessed this many a time in my dreams. The name of Jesus Christ and the blood of Jesus Christ gave me many victories in my dreams.

The Bible says those who call on the name of Jesus Christ shall be saved (Romans 10:13NKJV) and that we "overcame him, by the blood of the lamb and by the word of their testimony, and they loved not their lives unto the death" (Revelation 12:11 (KJV)).

It is also important to remember that the blood of Jesus Christ has a voice. It speaks. As stated in Hebrews 12:24, "and to Jesus the mediator of the new covenant, and to the blood of sprinkling, that speaks better things than that of Abel." The blood of anything, human and animals, speaks in the spirit realm, hence it is important for sacrifices, altars and covenants. Only the blood of Jesus Christ speaks better things for those who have received Jesus Christ and believe in His name. It is the voice of the blood of Jesus Christ that challenges any other voice, condemnation, accusations spoken in dreams.

The great thing about Jesus Christ is that because he lives, he mediates for the believers in the spirit realms in person and in the physical realms through the Holy Spirit. On the other hand, Satan only accuses and afflicts people; no mediation for those who are without Christ. Blood sacrifices at evil altars only speak evil to those who offer the sacrifices, and sometimes those evil covenants and transactions can be manifested after those who sacrificed at those altars are long dead. The thing is, Satan is a deceiver, and he can deceive the sacrificing generation into believing they are receiving good, such as fame, money, success, or whatever the sacrifice was for in their lifetime, awaiting them to die before he ravages their families for generations, wanting payback for whatever they have received. So those good things never really benefit people, especially if the next generations do not keep up with those sacrifices, altars and covenants. Dreams are best platforms to expose what the previous generations submitted, the spirits they served and covenants they forged while alive. As bible says, can a good tree produce bad fruit?

The dream realm is a spirit realm. If the human spirit is weak, it will not be able to combat anything the spirit realm plants in the life of that person when they are sleeping. The human spirit has a life of its own and needs to be fed good spiritual food to interact effectively in the spirit realm. For those who are in Christ, prayer, fasting, meditating on the word of God, the Bible and not the meditation of silence and yoga, reading the Bible daily, worshipping, praising God and living righteously is food to their spirit man. These holy acts are potent weapons in the spirit realms.

Those without Christ do many things. Some do transcendental meditation, yoga, demonic fasting and prayers, psychic readings, enchantments, repetitive prayers, worshipping creation, occultic practices such as illuminati and freemasonry, Satanic practices, consulting with spirit mediums, witchdoctors, priests, elders who are not with Christ and sacrificing and praying to idols in various religions of the world, reading stars and engaging with astrology, traditional and cultural practices, and many other thigs they do. In fact, anything that is done in the spirit realms outside the name and the blood of Jesus Christ and without the Holy Spirit is a Satanic practice and acts of witchcraft. Such do not help anyone when attacked in dreams as they pollute their spirit man.

Being able to see, hear, discern, speak and fight in the dream state is very crucial, and it is the work of the spirit man. Depending on how strong the person's spirit is, they can be subdued or overcome in their sleep. Most things we face are revealed or exposed in dreams.

Though dreams are important, the word of God is more important. It is only the word of God that can effectively cancel whatever tares the enemy plans and plants in people's lives when they are sleeping. Jesus Christ said in Matthew 13:25-26, "But when men slept, his enemy came and sowed tares and went his way, but when the grain had sprouted and produced a crop, then the tares also appeared." What the enemy plants can take a long time before it reveals itself as sickness, accidents, hardship, failure, addictions, divorce, death and many other unpleasant experiences. The Word of God is the sword of the Spirit that, when applied in the name of Jesus Christ, can destroy any tares planted by the devil in the night to destroy the person or groups of people. The blood of Jesus Christ cancels the evil covenants forged in the dream state because it is the blood of the new covenant.

Some things transition from the dream state to the physical within a short space of time, and sometimes they take longer. This makes praying immediately after the dream, when one gets up, even more important, speaking the word of God to either reject and cancel the dream or accept the dream and speak it to life while they still remember the dream clearly. The reason for praying immediately is that people typically forget most dreams over time. Praying about dreams can be done even for the dreams that come to mind from time past, as the Holy Spirit brings them to remembrance.

The spirit realms are not limited by time or space. The Holy Scriptures, The Bible, provide plenty of examples of the spiritual nature of physical life. The book of Ester gives a clear example of how a spiritual act can influence the physical outcome. In the book of Ester, when Mordecai, who was a Jew and worshipped only the true God, refused to reverence or bow to Haman, who was appointed by King Ahasuerus, believed to be the king of Persia, to sit above all princes that were with him. The king commanded that all the king's servants who were in the king's gate bow and reverenced Haman. Because Mordecai refused to do as the king commanded, Haman and his people decided to conspire and concoct a plan to get rid of all the Jews in every place ruled by King Ahasuerus. When Queen Ester came to know about Haman's plan through Mordecai, they decided to fast for 3 days so Queen Ester could intervene on behalf of the Jews to stop Haman. She succeeded because she first dealt with the issue in the spirit realms through fasting. In the end, it was Haman and his family that got killed instead of the Jews.

In fact, Haman was mocked twice. Before he took the place of the Jews in his cruel plan, the King could not sleep and asked for a book of records of the Chronicle to be read before him. It was found that Mordecai was the one who told about the plan to kill the king and was never honored. The king decided to honor Mordecai and asked Haman how the man who delighted the king should be honored. Haman thought the king was talking about him. He suggested an elaborate display of honor. After narrating the fitting honor, he was then commanded to do as he had spoken to Mordecai the Jew. This act was also instigated spiritually by disturbing the king's sleep.

The spirit realm was behind the physical preservation of the Jews in the physical realms by destroying Haman, whose plans to destroy Mordecai, and the Jews completely failed. Haman was killed by the same tools he had planned to kill Mordecai with. In return, Ester, Mordecai and the Jews became superior and mighty in the kingdom of King Ahasuerus because the unseen power of God was behind them through the obedience of Mordecai and Queen Esther.

PRAYER

Prayer is spirit. Praying is a formidable spiritual act. Many people in all the religions of the world profess and proclaim to pray. However, only one prayer counts. It is prayer in the name of Jesus Christ. That is why all sorts of prayers, audible or inaudible, including fasting, in the mighty name of our Lord and Savior Jesus Christ, offered in the power of the Holy Spirit and by faith, are irresistible, potent weapons. Prayer is a spiritual weapon so powerful and so creative in the hands of those who know how to offer it once they are born again. The Bible says that the weapons of our warfare are not carnal, they are mighty through God to the pulling down of strongholds, 2 Corinthians 10:4. These weapons are rooted in prayer aligned with the word of God.

A prayer that is not in the name of Jesus Christ as one's Lord and Savior, and not using the word of God, is weak and can easily fall into the category of what is called witchcraft prayer. The Bible says when we pray, we must do it in the name of Jesus Christ and by faith. The name of Jesus Christ gives believers authority in the spirit realm. It is the only name given unto man to connect with God. In Acts 4:12, it is written that "And there is salvation in no one else, for there is no other name under heaven given among men by which we must be saved."

In Philippians 2:9-11 it is written "Therefore God has highly exalted him and bestowed on him the name that is above every name, so that at the name of Jesus, every knee should bow, in heaven and on earth and under the earth, and every tongue confess that Jesus Christ is Lord, to the glory of God the father."

In John 14:13-14, Jesus said, "Whatever you ask in my name, this I will do, that the Father may be glorified in the Son. If you ask me anything in my name, I will do it."

In Mark 16:17, Jesus also said, "And these signs will accompany those who believe in my name. They will cast out demons and they will speak in new tongues."

1 Timothy 2:5 says, "For there is one God, and there is one mediator between God and men, the man Jesus Christ."

Colossians 1:16 and 3:17 says "For by him all things were created, in heaven and on earth, visible and invisible, whether thrones or dominions or rulers or authorities, all things were created through him and for him." "And whatever you do, in word or deed, do everything in the name of the Lord Jesus, giving thanks to God the Father through him." The name of Jesus Christ, called out by faith, is above sicknesses, life challenges, conditions, situations, the systems of this world and can make the impossible possible.

In John 10:30, Jesus Christ says, "I and the Father are one." When we pray in the name of Jesus Christ, we pray directly to the only God who created the heavens and the earth.

All these scripture verses testify that it is only in the name of Jesus Christ that prayer and any spiritual practice are holy and acceptable to God. Without Jesus Christ, any prayer and spiritual practice is a waste of time. Jesus Christ expresses this very well when he says in John 15:5 (KJV) "I am the vine, ye are the branches: He that abideth in me, and I in him, he bears much fruit. For without me ye can do nothing." It is very true that without Jesus Christ, things can fall apart hopelessly. With Jesus, there is hope and confidence. He gives spiritual power in the physical world.

Prayer is a spiritual language, and the blood of Jesus Christ is a currency in the spiritual realm. We are purchased by the blood of Jesus Christ shed at the cross for the remission of our sins and freedom from sin, death and Satan. The blood of Jesus Christ completes the transaction from death to life because it gives people the life of Jesus Christ, which is eternal life. The blood of Jesus Christ cleanses us and makes us righteous before God. The blood of Jesus Christ protects us and defends us from all evil. The blood of Jesus Christ also speaks better things in the lives of believers than anything that can ever be spoken or done against them. Invoking the blood of Jesus Christ through prayer is very critical.

There are many kinds of prayers a person can offer. There are prayers of healing, prayers of deliverance, prayers of supplication, prayers of thanksgiving, prayers of worship, prayers of intercession. There is one common denominator among them all. It is the name of Jesus Christ. The power of prayer and the blood of Jesus Christ are activated through faith. The level of faith one has determines the extent to which the person experiences that power. As it is written in Ephesians 3:8-12, 14-17 and 20, where Paul talks about the mystery of Christ so that the Gentiles should be fellow heirs, of the same body, and partakers of the promise of God in Christ through the gospel. Paul says, "To me, who am less than the least of all the saints, this grace was given, that I should preach among the Gentiles the unsearchable riches of Christ, and to make all see what is the fellowship of the mystery, which from the beginning of ages has been hidden in God who created all things through Jesus Christ, to the intent that now the manifold wisdom of God might be made known by the church to the principalities and powers in the heavenly places, according to the eternal purpose which He (God) accomplished in Christ Jesus our Lord in whom we have boldness and access with confidence through faith in him." "For this reason, I bow my knees to the Father of our Lord Jesus Christ, from whom the whole family in heaven and earth is named, that He would grant you, according to the riches of His glory, to be strengthened with might through His Spirit in the inner man, that Christ may dwell in your hearts through faith. "Now to Him who is able to do exceedingly abundantly above all that we ask or think, according to the power that works in us."

The power that works in us is the power of faith through the strengthening of the inner man by the Spirit of the living God.

THE WORD OF GOD

As Paul indicates, faith in Christ is the key, and Jesus Christ is the only access we have to God. It is very important to use the word of God to inform decisions and confess what we want to see in our lives. This includes the dream world. Speaking the word of God against unwanted things we saw and did in dreams when we wake up, reversing that which contradicted the word of God and agreeing and accepting that which aligned with the word of God, is more powerful than the dream. In Jeremiah 23:28-29 (KJV), it is written regarding the dreams and the Word of God: "The prophet that has a dream, let him tell a dream; and he that hath my word, let him speak my word faithfully. What is the chaff to the wheat? Saith the LORD. Is not my word like as a fire? Saith the LORD; and like a hammer that breaketh the rock in pieces?

The word of God is more powerful and important than any dream we can ever have at night or when we are sleeping. The reason is that the word of God written in the Bible is Spirit. Jesus Christ says in John 6:63 (NKJV), "It is the Spirit who gives life, the flesh profits nothing. The words that I speak to you are spirit and they are life." Because Jesus Christ is God and God is Spirit and Jesus Christ is the Word of God that created everything on earth, the words he speaks are spirit with authority in the spirit and physical realms. This is the case whether the word of God is spoken audibly, inaudibly or written down in the Bible. Jesus Christ and the Word of God are one, just as Jesus Christ and God are one.

In Hebrews 4:12 (KJV), it says, "For the word of God is quick and powerful, and sharper than any two-edged sword, and piercing even to the dividing asunder of soul and spirit, of both joints and marrow, and is a discerner of the thoughts and intents of the heart." This means that the word of God has the power to nullify anything one can ever see, say and do in any dream and can equally make those things that are good come to pass. The word of God can be declared for and against the dream. Knowing the word of God and confessing it regularly is necessary to achieve one's divine purpose and destiny and overcome both in the spirit and physical realms.

The Word of God is one of the weapons of warfare in the spiritual and physical realms. In 2 Corinthians 10:4 (KJV), it says, "For the weapons of our warfare are not carnal, but mighty through God to the pulling down of strongholds." Because the Word of God created everything on earth, everything on earth can never withstand the power of the Word of God. Everything submits to the Word of God spoken by faith. The word of God is also eternal.

Jesus Christ, who is God who came to the earth in the flesh, said all things on earth will pass away, but his words will never pass away. In Matthew 24:35 (NKJV), Jesus Christ said, "Heaven and earth will pass away, but my words will by no means pass away" God also said His words can never return to him without accomplishing what is has been sent to perform. In Isaiah 55:10-11 (NKJV) God said "For as the rain comes down, and the snow from heaven, and do not return there, but water the earth, and make it bring forth and bud, that it may give seed to the Sower and bread to the eater, so shall my word be that goes forth from my mouth; it shall not return to me void, but it shall accomplish what I please, and it shall prosper in the thing for which I sent it." This confirms that what the Bible says is surer than any theory, books used in other religions, extrabiblical books and texts, and the word spoken by the enemy.

FAITH

The word of God is a source for building faith in the minds and hearts of believers. It is a fountain from which a believer's faith flows. Faith built upon the word of God is a different kind of faith. Romans 10:17 (NKJV) says, "So then faith comes by hearing, and hearing by the word of God."

Hebrews 11:1 defines faith, saying, "Now faith is the substance of things hoped for, the evidence of things not seen."

Faith is a very dynamic force. Jesus Christ said, if you have faith as small as a mustard seed, you can move the mountains. Imagine how much a person with big faith can do and achieve if they put that faith to work.

Suffices to say God has given every living person an amount/a measure of faith, as expounded in Romans 12:3, to live on earth and make decisions and have confidence to pursue their purposes and desires. How and where a person chooses to apply their faith is their choice. Some people do not use their faith. In James 2:17 (NKJV), it says, "Thus also faith by itself, if it does not have works, is dead."

It says in the Bible that without faith no one can please God. As expounded in Hebrews 11:6 (NKJV), it says, "But without faith it is impossible to please him; for he who comes to God must believe that he is, and that he is a rewarder of those who diligently seek him."

If one has faith in God through Jesus Christ and by His Spirit, the light of God will work for them throughout their days on earth. With God, there are blessings and many other good things that God gives when we ask and pray by faith in the name of Jesus through His Spirit. The Bible says, "Every good and every perfect gift is from above, and comes down from the Father of lights, with whom there is no variation or shadow of turning, James 1:17.

It also says in Proverbs 10:22 that the blessing of the LORD makes one rich, and He adds no sorrow with it. This means when God blesses, those blessings can last generations and multiply instead of diminishing. These blessings are received by faith.

If one has faith in the darkness and what it offers through evil powers, demons, Satan and all his fallen angels and agents, darkness will work for them, though temporarily. However, with Satan, people only receive curses that can masquerade as good things. The consequences of those curses received disguised as excellent achievements can manifest in the lives of their descendants for generations long after their death. One might think that they have it good by putting their trust and faith in the darkness. This is a deception. Anything from Satan and darkness is temporary because the enemy, the thief, comes only to steal, to kill and to destroy, as stated in John 10:10. The results one receives by using darkness never last and bring sorrow because Satan has no friend and only gives to take something valuable from the receiver at a later stage or later generations.

As we have seen in the book of Genesis between Moses and Pharaoh, darkness could not compete with the light and the power of God operating in the lives of God's true servants and children. Pharaoh's magicians thought they could compete with Moses as he performed the miracles of God, but their confidence crashed after duplicating a few miracles through witchcraft sponsored by Satan and his demons and devils. Everything they did was temporary and could not be sustained. However, the miracles God brought through Moses were permanent. The magicians admitted to Pharaoh that Moses was working with the hand of God and were scared. Death came to take away what was most valuable in Egypt, the firstborn of everything from humans to animals. The magicians of Egypt came to respect and fear Moses. Whatever is from darkness brings sorrow and does not last. Something will come to erode that which is gained from darkness. Satan, the father of darkness and the thief, has no blessings to offer. His purpose is to steal, kill and destroy and not to bless. Only Jesus Christ gives blessings that last, as He came that we may have life and have it more abundantly (John 10:10)

However, in his infinite love and mercy, everyone, whether good or evil, benefits from the goodness of God if they apply their faith. Because God is Spirit and the spirit realm is legal, applying faith is a spiritual principle that God honors.

Every living being has faith that when they get up, the sun will shine, rain will come, night and day will come, air will be available, and they will experience the beauty of nature all over the world. These are just a few of those universal blessings every living being receives by faith. Because God has created everyone to be a free moral being with choices, some choose darkness while others choose the light. These choices can be at a personal level, family level, country level, continent level and world level. Every human choice, individually or collectively, is driven by some level of faith.

Nothing is without the influence of the spirit realm. Faith is a spirit. It is a currency in the spirit realms. No one, other than God, can see each person's faith. Faith can be enlarged. The more a person puts their faith to work, the more daring they become to face life and accomplish bigger things, whether it be a good thing in the light or an evil thing in darkness.

DARKNESS AND NIGHT

The dynamics of life are a mystery to many people who are not spiritually inclined or are operating from the flesh and therefore spiritually blind and are in darkness. Darkness is the absence of God, who is the light. It is darkness because it is deceptive, and the truth is not a part of it. People who patronize darkness in any way through myriads of practices, lifestyle and objects, are kept in the dark regarding the consequences of each action and choice or non-action. This is how most people become trapped in the deceptions of darkness, which sometimes disguise itself as light for generations through such things as success, fame, riches, power, position, influence and affluence. The light that shines in darkness deceives. Imagine a place that is unclean and poorly unkept under the disguise of the night lights. The place might look beautiful and appealing in the night but disgusting when the true light of the day comes. Darkness keeps people ignorant about what really matters because those leading them hide the truth. They provide what seems to be good, but the end thereof is destruction. The bibles in 1 Thessalonians 5:5 calls born-again Christians the children of the light and the children of the day, and not of the night nor of darkness. Those who are not in Christ are the children of the night and of darkness.

The light is called such because where there is light, nothing can be hidden, and everything is brought to the surface. The light brings freedom and power to those who are in the light. The light brings knowledge, wisdom, understanding, discernment and guidance. The most powerful person on earth is not the president of the country, the CEO of a big company, the CEOs of organizations or even the rich and famous people. The most powerful people are the ones who walk in the light of Jesus Christ, know and understand the power they have by believing in Jesus Christ. As it is written in Mark 16: 17-18, Jesus said "And these signs shall follow them that believe; in my name shall they cast out devils; they shall speak with new tongues; they shall take up serpents; and if they drink any deadly thing, it shall not hurt them; they shall lay hands on the sick, and they shall be healed." There is spiritual power that can never be taken away by anything or anyone from those who walk in the light of Jesus Christ. No fame, riches, power, influence and affluence can buy these things. However, anointed, spiritually powerful Christians can still have fame, riches, power, influence and affluence. I believe a true Christian, who truly believes and lives by faith, worships God in spirit and in truth, filled with the Holy Spirit, is the most powerful person on earth. This makes life a mystery.

LIFE IS A SPIRITUAL ENIGMA

Life is a mystery and all spiritual. It is important to remember that Jesus Christ is life. Everything living comes from him, through him and by him. The spiritual nature of life makes it a puzzle. As stated before, everything in life starts in the spirit realm and manifests in the physical realm at some point. The creation of the Earth is a good example. The earth was without form, the Holy Spirit was hovering around, and God, who is Spirit, spoke and whatever He spoke, manifested on earth. It is a puzzle that words have such creative powers. It means words are spirit(s), whether audible or inaudible.

In Genesis 1:2-3, it says, "And the earth was without form and void; and darkness was upon the face of the deep. And the Spirit of God moved upon the face of the waters, and God said, "Let there be light," and there was light."

The earth was created by the Word, and that Word is Jesus Christ. That is why we say words are powerful and creative. People curse with words and bless with words. The tongue is such a small member of the body, and capable of doing greater things, good or evil. In James 3:5 and 8-10 (NKJV), it says, "Even so the tongue is a little member and boasts great things. See how great a forest/matter a little fire kindles." Again, it says in verses 8-10, "But no man can tame the tongue. It is an unruly evil, full of deadly poison. With it we bless our God and Father, and with it we curse men, who have been made in the similitude of God. Out of the same mouth proceed blessing and cursing. My brethren, these things ought not to be so."

Spiritual people, those connected to the spirit realm, whether it be a connection with darkness or with the true light, Jesus Christ, can call whatever has already happened in the spirit into the physical realm or cause things to happen in the spirit realm so they can manifest them in the physical realm using words.

For a born-again Christian to be a spiritual being, it started in the Garden of Eden when humanity became spiritually dead through sin, followed by the prophecies given by the prophets of the old in the Old Testament hundreds of years before Jesus Christ was born, then his physical birth, then his earthly life, death, resurrection and ascension into heaven. It is a transforming process to move from curses to blessings and it involves words. A Christian receives the salvation mystery through words, confessing with the mouth and believing in the heart that Jesus Christ is one's Lord and Savior. This is followed by baptismal through immersion in the water and not sprinkling of water on the head of an infant. This is then followed by the filling of the Holy Spirit and receiving the baptism of fire of the Holy Spirit that only Jesus Christ gives. Both water and fire baptism are mysteries as they change a person's spiritual garment and empower them to function effectively and legally in the spirit realms. Once a person becomes a born-again Christian, they receive dual residency, one in heaven and one on earth at the same time, and their lives are lived in Christ Jesus.

Ephesians 2:1-6 (NKJV) says, "And you he made alive, who were dead in trespasses and sins, in which you once walked according to the course of this world, according to the prince of the power of the air (Satan, devils, demons), the spirit who now works in the sons/children of disobedience, among whom also we all once conducted ourselves in the lusts of our flesh, fulfilling the desires of the flesh and of mind, and were by nature children of wrath, just as the others. But God, who is rich in mercy, because of his great love with which he loved us, even when we were dead in trespasses, made us alive together with Christ (by grace you have been saved), and raise us up together (with Christ), and made us sit together in heavenly places in Christ Jesus, that in ages to come he might show the exceeding riches of his grace in his kindness toward us in Christ Jesus." It is a spiritual mystery for one to be a Christian. People on earth see a born-again Christian as another human being, but the spirit beings and those who practice in darkness see a different person.

Once a person becomes a Christian, they become changed because their lives are lived through Jesus Christ. They become a new creation, born again by the blood of Jesus Christ and the Spirit of the living God. They become the habitation of the Holy Spirit. They stop being the commanders of their own lives. The Holy Spirit, the fire with which Jesus Christ baptizes born-again Christians, becomes their helper, comforter, defender, protector, wisdom and many other benefits of being a child of God. It is only once the people are born again that they become the children of God.

Everyone is a creation of God, but not everyone is a child of God. Before anyone is born again, they are the children of their biological, physical mothers and fathers. But once born again, God becomes the Father. This is a spiritual exchange. It is only true believing Christians who are born again who become both spiritual and physical beings at the same time.

This is a mystery.

Those who are not born again, even if they go to a Christian church, pray and read the Bible, are not really the children of God because they did not confess with their mouth and believe in their hearts that Jesus Christ is their personal Lord and Savior.

Jesus Christ is the only way to God, as He himself is God, who appeared and came in the flesh, taking a human form so He can reconcile us to Himself. When a person becomes born again, they enter a covenant sealed by the blood of Jesus Christ as a sacrifice shed at the altar of the cross of Calvary over 2000 years ago, but always new and fresh each day. This covenant is spiritual and gives Christians legal access into the spiritual realm and to the heavenly throne of God. The cross of Jesus Christ is the highest, everlasting altar, where the last blood sacrifice was offered. The blood shed at the cross speaks for Christians in the physical and spiritual realms.

The day-to-day living of a true Christian, a true child of God, becomes a manifestation of this spiritual covenant in the physical realm. Truly, without the gospel, no one can know God at a personal level and understand this mystery.

All the other religions of the world, which deny Jesus Christ or believe he was just a prophet, deny his deity can never enter the Kingdom of God. The religions of the world outside of Jesus Christ are all pagan and idol worship. Some worship the crescent moon, some worship spiritual gurus who claim to have received revelations from spirit beings who are basically demons and fallen angels who taught them basically what qualifies as witchcraft, some worship a million gods for each aspect in their lives, some worship creation and created objects, as well as many other things. This is because at the deepest level, man is created to worship in the spirit realm and craves inner spiritual connection with a being higher than himself.

Believing in Jesus Christ is the only access human beings have to the Kingdom of God. Jesus Christ is the key and the only way to God. Jesus Christ said in John 14:6 (NKJV) that "I am the way, the truth and the life; no one comes to the Father except through me." Believing in Jesus Christ qualifies human beings to be called the children of God, as written in John 1:12 that "…as many as received Him, to them He gave the right to become children of God, to those who believe in His name." In Galatians 3:26, it says people become children of God through faith in Christ Jesus. This tells us that many people around the world – created in His image, who pray to other deities or other things – are not the children of God, even if they pray and say "God" in their prayers.

There is no deity other than Jesus Christ who can create a human being and the earth. Other deities are created beings, basically demons, spirit beings and man-made images, and are all the schemes of the devil to keep humanity in darkness. Many people unknowingly pray to the devil, who has deceived them through the myriad religious choices and spiritual practices, because he can transform himself into a false light. The Bible says in 2 Corinthians 11:14 that "And no wonder! For Satan himself transforms himself into an angel of light." He disguises himself as the light, but he is the false light. Those who are without Christ, practicing any kind of religion and spiritual activity, are following the false light.

When a Christian prays by faith in the name of Jesus Christ by the power of the Holy Spirit, their prayers reach the throne room of the righteous God, and God answers their prayers. Prayer, whether audible or inaudible, is a spiritual act of faith that brings and manifests things and experiences into the physical life. Jesus Christ is the righteousness of Christians. And Christians approach the throne room of God by prayer through the righteousness of Jesus Christ. Without the name of Jesus Christ, His blood, and the Holy Spirit, there is no power to break through in the spirit realm. A prayer offered without the name of Jesus Christ, even if it gets "answered," provides no certainty that God has answered that prayer, since the devil can deceive people into thinking that God has answered their prayers. If it is not in the name of Jesus, Satan could be the one responding, and he has no good thing to offer. Whatever you get, he will come back to collect from you even more than you got. There will be something that will cost you. The Bible says that the "blessings of the Lord maketh one rich and are without sorrow." Proverbs 10:22 (KJV). With Satan, sorrow and pain could well be in the package of what looks like an answered prayer and a blessing.

Those in the dark realms have their own ways, sponsored by the devil and evil spirits, to operate in the spirit and manifest things in the physical realms. Any access into the spirit realm not granted by the Holy Spirit and without the name and the blood of Jesus is dangerous and unsafe. It is basically illegal. The spirit realm is a legal realm, a realm ruled by covenants, altars, and sacrifices. For example, the crucifixion of Jesus Christ has established the cross of Calvary as an altar in heaven and earth for Christians. The blood shed at the cross of Calvary was the blood sacrifice for Christians, and the crucified body of Jesus Christ and the blood that was spilled established an eternal covenant with God for Christians. The altar of Christ is ruled by the Holy Spirit, the Spirit of the living God that Jesus Christ promised to send to those who believe and give to those who are born again. As Jesus Christ told Nicodemus in John 3:3, 5, 6, 7, and 8 that "except a man be born again, he cannot see the kingdom of God. Except a man be born of water and of Spirit, he cannot enter into the kingdom of God. That which is born of the flesh is flesh, and that which is born of the Spirit is spirit. You must be born again. The wind blows where it wishes, and you hear the sound of it, but cannot tell where it comes from and where it goes. So is everyone who is born of the Spirit."

THE HOLY SPIRIT

The Holy Spirit is the third person in the Holy Trinity. He is the one helping Christians live a Christian life and restricting the devil from fully operating on earth. As written in 2 Thessalonians 2:7 (NKJV), "For the mystery of lawlessness is already at work; only He who now restrains will do so until He is taken out of the way." The restrainer is the Holy Spirit. He was the first to come on earth, and I believe He would be the last to leave the earth. This verse implies that the Holy Spirit will at some point be taken out of the way. When this happens, lawlessness will rule freely on earth.

The Holy Spirit is the one who convicts people of sin and helps them to be saved through Christ. He is the one who teaches humanity about Jesus Christ, helps people understand and come to the faith and reveals the mysteries of the relationship between the spiritual and the physical realms. Jesus Christ is the one who sends the Holy Spirit into people and baptizes believers with the Holy Spirit's fire. For believers to receive and be baptized in the Holy Spirit, Jesus Christ had to leave so he could send the Holy Spirit to be with believers.

Jesus Christ, as a person, could only be in a specific place at a time. However, the Holy Spirit is everywhere at the same time, seeing everything that happens on earth, including people and their inner most secrets and knows what will happen at every second. He is the Spirit of power, revelation, wisdom, knowledge and understanding, helping believers all over the world. Because Jesus Christ is God, the Holy Spirit is the spirit of Jesus Christ, and he testifies about Jesus Christ. God Almighty, Jesus Christ, and the Holy Spirit are one, the same person. In John 16:7-8 (KJV), Jesus said, "It is expedient for you that I go away, for if I go not away, the Comforter will not come unto you; but if I depart, I will send him to you. And when He has come, He will convict the world of sin, and of righteousness and of judgment."

The Holy Spirit is also called the Helper, the Advocate, Intercessor, and the Teacher who walks with all those who are born again. Jesus said in John 16:13 (KJV), that "Howbeit when He, the Spirit of truth is come, he will guide you into all truth, for He shall not speak of himself; but whatsoever He shall hear, that shall He speak; and He will shew you things to come." The Holy Spirit is also the Spirit of prophecy, as He tells Christians what is to come. He is also the Spirit of revelation, as He is the revealer of all truth and even of things that are done in secret.

In 1 Corinthians 2:7-10, it says, "But we speak the wisdom of God in a mystery, even the hidden wisdom which God ordained before the ages for our glory; which none of the princes/rulers of this age knew; for had they known it, they would not have crucified the Lord of glory. But as it is written, 'Eye has not seen, nor ear heard, nor have entered into the heart of man, the things which God has prepared for those who love Him'. But God has revealed them to us through His Spirit. For the Spirit searches all things, yes, the deep things of God."

In Psalms 139:7, it says, "Where can I hide from your Spirit? Or where can I flee from Your presence? If I ascend into heaven, You are there; If I make my bed in hell, behold, You are there. If I take the wings of the morning, and dwell in the uttermost parts of the sea, even there, Your hand shall lead me, and your right hand shall hold me." The Holy Spirit is all-present, all-knowing, and all-seeing. Nothing can ever be hidden from the Holy Spirit. He is everywhere all the time; on earth, in heaven, under the earth, and in the sea.

Other spirits like the devil, his demons, and fallen angels cannot be present everywhere all the time. They are not able to do that because they are created beings. That is why they use such things as monitoring spirits, dream attacks, pollution, human possession, and deceptions to capture, occupy, and inhibit humanity. Only the Holy Spirit of God, the Spirit of Jesus Christ can be present everywhere, all-knowing, and all-powerful, and all seeing. He only comes to dwell in the lives of those who give their lives to Jesus Christ, and only those who ask for him get baptized in his fire, which helps believers live a holy life.

The opposite is true of all the other spirits. They implant themselves in the lives of people, families, nations, systems, and institutions for their evil purposes by force and trickery. Although the Holy Spirit helps humanity to live on earth, He does not dwell in everyone, or walks with everyone. Human beings are free to choose whether they want the Holy Spirit in their personal life as a helper, teacher, defender, protector, advocate, wisdom, righteousness, and many other things he does in the lives of those who receive him.

Romans 8:26-27 (NKJV), says, "Likewise the Spirit also helps in our weaknesses. For we do not know what we should pray for as we ought, but the Spirit Himself makes intercession for us with groanings which cannot be uttered. Now he who searches the hearts knows what the mind of the Spirit is, because he makes intercession for the saints according to the will of God."

People who practice things like meditation of all sorts from other religious practices, yoga, demonic prayers, levitation, astral traveling, projections, and many other spiritual practices can enter the spirit realm where they get to interact with the spirit beings, which are devils, Satan, fallen angels, and demons. This is because their practices are a form of worship, not of God, but of contrary spirits. They may call those evil and contrary spirits "gurus," "spirit guides," "angels," "prophets," "god" of this and that, the "gods," "ancestors," "queen mother," "queen of heaven," or whatever name they ascribe to them. These spirit beings can disguise themselves as the light and mislead people who follow them.

Because unbelievers do not have the name of Jesus Christ, the blood of Jesus Christ, and the Holy Spirit, their entry in the spirit realm is illegal and dangerous. In the end, without Jesus Christ, Satan, the prince of this world, is the spirit people submit to, whether they know it or not, or whether they think what they are doing is good or not. These religious practices are of darkness; what they practice is false worship, and where they worship become their altars, evil altars. Their activities at those altars are sacrifices offered to whatever spirit is behind those altars, and at those altars, they establish evil covenants with those spirits. The Bible calls these spirits "idols that cannot hear or understand." It is idolatry, the worship of an image, object, creation, or a person as God instead of the true God. It really does not matter what the name of the religion is, how popular it is, or what it does to claim holiness, it is of the devil and leads people into the broad path to destruction and hell.

Behind every idol, there is an evil spirit. It is the evil spirit in an idol that deceives its worshippers. In the end, all evil spirits are destructive and do the works of Satan, who desired to be worshipped and is jealous of God. This is well articulated in Isaiah 14:12-15 (NKJV), that says, "How you are fallen from heaven, O Lucifer, son of morning. How you are cut down to the ground, you who weakened the nations. For you have said in your heart, I will ascend into heaven, I will exalt my throne above the stars of God, I will also sit on the mount of the congregation on the farthest sides of the north, I will ascend above the heights of the clouds, I will be like the Most High." Yet you shall be brought down to Sheol, to the lowest depths of the Pit." It is believed that Sheol is the place of the dead or hell.

It is important to note that in Isaiah 14, Satan did not vocalize his intentions but thought them out. God hears our thoughts just as he hears our spoken words.

Bottom line: Satan is not God and will never be God. He weakens people to worship him so they can receive the same judgment he has already received and join him in the lowest depths of the pit already prepared for him. He is the spirit working in the hearts and minds of those who reject Jesus Christ. Jesus also told us in John 16:7-11 that the prince of this world is already judged. He said, "Nevertheless, I tell you the truth; It is expedient for you that I go away; for if I go not away, the Comforter will not come unto you; but if I depart, I will send him unto you. And when he is come, he will reprove/convict the world of sin, and of righteousness and of judgment, of sin because they believe not on me; of righteousness because I go to my Father, and you see me no more; of judgment because the prince of this world is judged."

Not believing that Jesus Christ is the Son of God who came in the flesh for the remission of humanity's sins and rejecting him as the perfect sacrifice of God and as the Messiah is a sin before God, because it makes God a liar. The Comforter is the Holy Spirit whom Jesus sends to the believers. Jesus was telling that it is important that he be crucified and rise again for the sake of humanity, so people can be saved and be rescued from the judgment Satan and demons have already received.

Only Jesus Christ, by His Spirit, leads people on the narrow path that leads to life eternal in heaven. In Matthew 7:13 (NKJV), Jesus Christ says, "Enter by the narrow gate; for wide is the gate and broad is the way that leads to destruction, and there are many who go in by it." In the New Living Translation (NLT), it says, "You can enter God's Kingdom only through the narrow gate. The highway to hell is broad, and its gate is wide for the many who choose that way." The broad highway means the varied ways and means Satan uses to mislead and misguide people, with lots of options and choices that take people to hell. Only Jesus Christ is the way to God, the truth of God, and the life of God.

The mysterious nature of life requires everyone to be more aware of the state of their inner being and the external environment they allow and interact with. The spirit realm that influences people's lives, choices, decisions, and experiences works from the inside out because humans are spirits clothed in mortal bodies. Thoughts, desires, and emotions are products of and influenced by the spirit realm. When we act on those thoughts, desires, and emotions, we are submitting to some spiritual being, and that could be the evil spirit or the Holy Spirit.

Life is dynamic and never straightforward. There are also no coincidences in life. We experience life based on what has happened before our time, as is the case with the sin of Adam and Eve, or what we or someone has spoken or done, such as parents and family, or what we desire and think, such as our personal ambitions, whether consciously or unconsciously.

GENERATIONAL BLESSINGS AND CURSES

Today everyone, including newborn children, have the sin of disobedience from Adam and Eve and the consequences of that sin as an inheritance. Their act of disobedience was a spiritual doorway for sin to enter the world and for Satan to enter and control humans and their affairs. When Satan approached Eve, he had a spiritual goal to achieve, which was to capture and take over God's creation and the earthly dominion God gave humanity through Adam. That is why the Bible says that all creation is groaning, waiting for its deliverance. The devil needed Adam and Eve to just sin once. He knew that God is Holy and their sin of disobedience would be enough to separate man from God and from His light, therefore dying spiritually, living in darkness in the world controlled by Satan. Man was given dominion over everything on the earth at creation. Adam and Eve's sin caused man to lose that dominion. This was the beginning of generational curses.

At creation, man was given generational blessings. Believing in and confessing Jesus Christ as one's personal Lord and Savior, and calling on His name, is the only way to regain what was lost.

Human beings need the spiritual savior to overcome spiritually and physically. The thing is, God is Spirit, and humans relate to God from their spiritual position. This is also true of Satan. He is a spirit, a created angel who was a cherub. He also relates to people from their spiritual position. This is why he has established a myriad of ways and methods of worshipping for people to choose from. This includes false religions of the world and practices that are in darkness, including lifestyle choices. He is looking for worship. So, when people in various places do, say, and think what he wants, they are fulfilling his ambitions. However, he will never attain his ambitions because he can never be like the Most High.

Even in families, what the predecessors have done tends to have a tremendous impact on the lives of people in those families. This is even worse if the individuals in families choose to continue in the paths of their predecessors which were characterized by sin, iniquities, and transgression against God. Romans 3:23-24 says, "For all have sinned and fall short of the glory of God, and all are justified freely by his grace through the redemption that came by Christ Jesus."

Exodus 20:4-6 says, "You shall not make for yourself an image in the form of anything in heaven above or on the earth beneath or in the waters below. You shall not bow to them or worship them; for I the Lord your God, am a jealous God, punishing the children for the sins of their parents to the third and fourth generation of those that hate me, but showing love to a thousand generations of those who love me and keep my commandment."

Choosing Jesus Christ in any generation reverses the curses for a thousand generations in a family or nations. Because of His love and mercy, God has made a way for everyone. In Isaiah 43:7, God says, "Everyone who is called by my name, whom I have created for my glory, whom I formed and made. Bring all who claim me as their God, for I have made them for my glory. It was I who created them." This creation is through Jesus Christ. We become children of God when we put our faith in Jesus Christ. We are then called by His name and receive generational blessings.

In Exodus 34:7, God says, "I lavish unfailing love to a thousand generations. I forgive iniquity, rebellion, and sin." When people humble themselves and ask God for forgiveness, God is faithful to forgive. Any person who says they have not sinned, when even a newborn has sinned are driven by self-righteousness. It is pride and arrogance to claim such righteousness. Pride and arrogance are evil spirits. The Bible says, "All have sinned and fall short of the glory of God." (Romans 3:23, (NKJV)) Humanity needs forgiveness from God.

It is through the blood of Jesus Christ that this forgiveness is achieved. The blood of Jesus Christ washes away all sins. God even forgives witchcraft and idolatry when people repent and seek his forgiveness. Idolatry is an iniquity. The Bible says that rebellion is the sin of witchcraft and God hates witchcraft. It is such a serious transgression that He says, "You shall suffer not a witch to live" (Exodus 22:18). However, when an idolater or a witch chooses Jesus Christ, their sins get washed away by the blood of Jesus Christ, and they are received in the family and the Kingdom of God. The blood of Jesus Christ also breaks all generational curses and introduces a new foundation in the lives of people and families anchored by Christ Jesus and His Holy Spirit.

However, for those who remain in their sins, they disadvantage their kids and generations to come. God, in Exodus 34:7, continues to say, "He will in no way clear the guilty, visiting the iniquity of the fathers on the children and children's children, to the third and fourth generation." Refusing Jesus Christ when a person knows the truth is very evil because not only does that person suffers, but innocent children inherit a spiritually handicapped life and bear the consequences of their fathers and mothers who refused Jesus Christ. Refusing Jesus Christ and rejecting the gospel of Jesus Christ perpetuates generational curses.

Believing in Jesus Christ is a spiritual inheritance of blessings for generations. Even a poor person can leave their descendants an inheritance of blessings here on earth if they are with Christ. Salvation cannot be bought because God is a fair and just God, a respecter of no persons and all humans are equal in the sight of God. Therefore, salvation is equally available to the rich and poor, the educated and uneducated, Jews and Gentiles, and to all people of all races. It is a gift from God and therefore a sin when people refuse to believe in Jesus Christ through whom humanity receives salvation. As written in Isaiah 55:1, "Ho! Everyone who thirsts, come to the waters; And you who have no money, come buy and eat. Yes, come, buy wine and milk without money and without price." Salvation is free to all who believe in Jesus Christ, the giver of the living waters.

Numbers 14:18 says, "The LORD is slow to anger, abounding in love and forgiving sin and rebellion. Yet he does not leave the guilty unpunished; he punishes the children for the sin of parents to the third and fourth generation." Isaiah 14:21 says, "Prepare slaughter for his children for the iniquity of their fathers; that they do not possess the land, nor fill the face of the world with cities." The sufferings we see in the world are the outcome of someone's decision not to repent. The good thing is, anyone in any place can choose to repent and put their faith in Jesus Christ to reverse the judgment issued due to the sins of predecessors. Generational curses do not have to persist from generation to generation.

Everything that happens has already happened in the spirit realm. Ancestors sinned in the past and the judgment was issued in the past. The current generation is suffering not necessarily due to fresh sins, transgressions, and iniquities. The unfortunate thing is that not everyone needs to sin in a community of people or family. Just one person sinning is enough to cause curses to work and everyone in that community or family to suffer the consequences of sin, resulting from curses. It is only by being born again of the Spirit of the living God and receiving deliverance in the name of Jesus Christ that those generational curses, including the sin of Adam and Eve that caused all humanity to be born in sin, and the related curses, can be broken, and a new foundation in Christ to be established. The key is that though salvation is personal, the presence of a saved person in the community or family can help to preserve unsaved people.

Imagine if no one ever repents, like in Sodom and Gomorrah. The sufferings will be perpetual until a generation comes that will hear the calling of God and choose to obey the voice calling them to repentance. There are nations that are no more because of their unrepentant sins, transgressions, and iniquities. They are extinct. There are families that have vanished from the face of the earth because of unrepentant sins. Unrepentant sins can cause barrenness in people and without heirs, the family line can be extinct.

In his infinite mercies and because He loves His creation, God made a way for the children to renounce the sins of predecessors in their family lines and take on a new life in Christ. This allows people to receive the inheritance prepared for those who would be childlike to believe the completed work of the cross of Jesus Christ at Calvary. Once a person comes to know and receive Jesus Christ, it is important that they teach their children the way of the Lord. Proverbs 22:6 (NKJV), says, "Train up a child in the way he should go, and when he is old, he will not depart from it."

The God who brings salvation in nations or families will see to it that the blessings remain even up to a thousand generations. Jeremiah 31:28-34 (NKJV) says, "And it shall come to pass, that as I have watched over them, to pluck up, and to break down, and to throw down, and to destroy, and to afflict; so will I watch over them, to build and to plant, says the LORD. In those days they shall say no more: "The fathers have eaten sour grape, and the children's teeth are set at edge. But every man shall die for his own iniquity, every man who eats the sour grapes, his teeth shall be set on edge. Behold, the days are coming, says the LORD, when I will make a new covenant with the house of Israel and with the house of Judah, not according to the covenant that I made with their fathers in the day that I took them by the hand to lead them out of the land of Egypt, My covenant which they broke, though I was a husband to them, says the LORD. But this shall be the covenant that I will make with the house of Israel after those days, says the LORD: I will put My law in their minds, and write it on their hearts, and I will be their God, and they shall be My people." This passage of the scripture applies to those who put their faith in Jesus Christ, as the Bible calls them the "Israel of God." Galatians 6:15-16 says, "For in Christ Jesus neither circumcision (Jews) nor uncircumcision (Gentiles) avails anything, but a new creation. And as many as walk according to this rule, peace and mercy be upon them, and upon the Isreal of God."

In the new covenant that God has with His children through the blood of Jesus Christ, children do not have to endure the consequences of the sins, afflictions, transgressions, and iniquities of their fathers, mothers, and ancestors. If a parent or a child chooses Jesus Christ and enters a new covenant, they become a new creation and redefine the destinies of those who come after them. In the Old Testament, this was demonstrated by the Israelites who wandered 40 years in the wilderness, and never entered the promised land except Joshua and Caleb who believed God. The rest did not enter because it was a generation of unbelieving, complaining, and disobedient people. In Deuteronomy 1:34-36 (NKJV), Moses said to that generation: "And the LORD heard the sound of your words, and he was angry and swore an oath, saying

"Surely not one of these men of evil generation shall see that good land of which I swore to give to your fathers, except Caleb the son of Jephunneh, he shall see it, and to him and his children I am giving the land on which he walked, because he wholly followed the LORD." I believe the demise of that generation was a deliverance from what could have become a generational curse for the next generation. Their death in the wilderness was God's mercy for the generation that was able to enter the promised land.

God is a God of generations. People can break generational curses and start enjoying generational blessings through Jesus Christ. They can pray to God to save their souls and those of their children, receiving the grace of salvation and the love of God for a thousand generations.

Ezekiel 18:19-20 also elaborates on this, stating, "Yet you say, 'why should the son not bear the guilt of the father?' Because the son has done what is lawful and right, and has kept all My statutes and observed them, he shall surely live. The soul who sins shall die. The son shall not bear the guilt of the father, nor the father bear the guilt of the son. The righteousness of the righteous shall be upon himself, and the wickedness of the wicked shall be upon himself."

Through Jesus Christ, people are individually saved by grace, and the righteousness of Jesus becomes their righteousness. When the saved teach their children the way of salvation, the seed of generational blessings is planted. Through the generations, that seed geminates and produce good fruits, descendants who walk in the ways of God and see the goodness of God in the land of the living.

Acts 16:31 emphasizes this, saying, "Believe on the Lord Jesus Christ, and you will be saved, you and your household." One repentant soul in the family can be the reason the whole household receives the grace of salvation. Even in the case of Sodoma and Gomorrah, God said to Abraham, if He were to find a few righteous souls, he would preserve the city. Unfortunately, wickedness was the order of the day, and the city was destroyed by God.

2 Corinthians 5:17-18 (NKJV), says, "Therefore, if anyone is in Christ, he is a new creation; old things have passed away, behold, all things have become new. Now all things are of God, who has reconciled us to Himself through Jesus Christ, and has given us the ministry of reconciliation, that this, that God was in Christ, reconciling the world to Himself, not imputing their trespasses to them, and has committed to us the word of reconciliation." God came to earth through Christ, not to judge the world but to point the world to the truth and reconcile humanity to Himself.

We live in a dispensation of grace that God gives for humanity to escape hell.

LIFE AND DEATH

As people, we go through various stages, ideally from newborn to old age, and the length of days on earth is only known to God. The path is not always that predictable. Some people leave this earth prematurely for several reasons. I believe every premature death is the work of the devil, capitalizing on some iniquity in their families or in a person's life to afflict a person with premature death. The iniquity could be from generational disobedience. The Bible says that the wages of sin is death. This tells us that human beings die because of sin. As we know by now, Proverbs 26:2 says, "A curse causeless shall not come."

However, those that are in and with Jesus Christ only go to sleep to wait for the day of the Lord at his second coming, to be raised and live with Christ, ruling the nations in the New Jerusalem. Their soul and spirit go to heaven to be in the presence of God. People who are saved by confessing with their mouth and believing in their heart that Jesus Christ is the Son of God don't really die. They continue to live in heaven. In the presence of God, who is life, there cannot be death. Jesus Christ said He is the way, the truth and the life. Following the ways and the truth of the gospel, the good news of Jesus Christ, brings life and destroys death.

Those who have rejected salvation through Christs when they were alive or are without Christ at the point of death, when their time ends on earth, they go to hell, meaning that their souls go to hell where there are torments and gnashing of teeth, while their spirit, which belongs to God, goes back to God. They are not born again, renewed and brought to life by the Spirit of the living God. Their lives remain in sin as everyone on earth is born in sin and death is the wage of the sin that everyone is born into. Only by being born again and repenting, the old garment of sin and the wages of sin, which is death can be removed. Then a person qualifies to be written in the Book of Life. Repentance is not a one-time confession people make at the point of the new birth in Christ. It is a daily thing, because even those that are born again are not immune to sin. People sin with their thoughts, actions, and words more regularly than they care to admit. This is why the Lord's Prayer in Matthew 6:12 says, "Forgive us our trespasses as we forgive those that trespass against us." This means that we ought to be forgiven daily by God and forgive others who wrong us on a regular basis. I believe the Lord's Prayer should be a Christian's daily prayer.

For those that are not repentant, refuse to repent, refuse to believe in Jesus Christ and salvation through Christ Jesus, and therefore not born again, at the end of the final judgment, they will have their part in the lake of fire with Satan, demons, death, the grave, and all evil spirits, which will be their second death, because their names will not be found in the Book of Life.

In Revelation 20:12-14 (NKJV) it says, "And I saw the dead, small and great, stand before God (the throne of God); and the books were opened. And another book was opened, which is the Book of Life. And the dead were judged according to their works, by the things which were written in the books. The sea gave up the dead that were in it, and death and hell (hades) delivered up the dead who were in them. And they were judged, each one according to his works. Then death and hell (hades) were thrown into the lake of fire. This is the second death." Death and the grave are spirits, just like other evil spirits.

In Revelation 21:7-8 (NKJV) it says, "He who overcomes shall inherit all things; and I will be his God, and he shall be my son. But the cowardly (fearful), unbelieving, abominable (corrupt), murderers (those who hate their brothers and are angry with their brothers and sisters without a cause), sexually immoral, sorcerers (those who practice witchcraft and rebellious people), idolaters (idol worshippers and stubborn people), and all liars shall have their part in the lake which burn with fire and brimstone, which is the second death."

The Bible says in 1 Samuel 15:23 that "For rebellion is as the sin of witchcraft and stubbornness is an iniquity and idolatry. Because you have rejected the word of the LORD, He also has rejected you from being king." Rejecting the word of God, who is Jesus Christ, is a sin that lands people into eternal torment. In 1 John 3:15 it says, "Whoever hates his brother is a murderer, and you know that no murderer has eternal life abiding in him." Jesus also said in Matthew 5:21-22 (KJV) that "You have heard that it was said to those of old, 'You shall not murder, and whoever murders will be in danger of the judgment'. But I say to you that whoever is angry with his brother without a cause shall be in danger of judgement."

The sins that will cause second death are very widespread and noticeable in the world today. There is so much hatred in the world, even among family members. People have become more rebellious, hating things they used to hold sacred, such as the nuclear family, the gospel, and Christianity. Sexual immorality has become a lifestyle and a standard in all age groups. It is not uncommon today to find a sexually active 12-year-old or less. Sexual immorality includes same sex relationships and marriages, sex changes/transgenderism and all the other practices that go with it. Such sins are out of control and celebrated through such things as pride parades the world over. Killing, including abortions, has also increased. People are openly practicing witchcraft and sorcery in many areas of life, mainly in the name of pagan worship, tradition, culture, spirituality, and Halloween, rejecting God. Many have walked away from the truth that is only found in Christ. Unbelief and pressure to be inclusive and embrace diversity have driven many to focus on the self, even coming up with new ways to self-express with pronouns, expecting people to oblige even if it contradicts and challenges the established ways. There are government policies and regulations which strive to accommodate and promote abominable things and practices in societies. Corruption and lies have become the norm, even from the previously trusted and reliable institutions. The explosion of social media has made access to the masses easy to start protests and revolutions, and one never know what and who is true and false on those platforms.

In the Christian church, there are many who would qualify as false teachers and prophets (liars) teaching strange doctrines and doing strange miracles. Some even mix Jesus Christ with their practices of darkness. There are previously trusted ministers in the church who have been exposed to practice sexual immoralities, witchcraft, occultist practices, and are in secret societies. Today, not everyone who says "Jesus" means the Jesus of the Bible. The environment makes it challenging even for born-again Christians. It is important to hold on to the word of God, discerning spirits by the help of the Holy Spirit to overcome and never face the second death. In Matthew 24:24 (NKJV), Jesus Christ says, "For false Christ's and false prophets will arise and show great signs and wonders to deceive, if possible, even the elect."

Jesus said in Matthew 7:22 (NIV) that "Many will say to Me in that day (on judgment day) 'Lord, Lord, did we not prophesy in Your name, in Your name drive out demons, and in Your name perform many miracles?'. And then I will declare to them, 'I never knew you; depart from Me, you who practice lawlessness!'. Truly, lawlessness, sometimes in the name of innovation, creativity, keeping up with the times, religious practices, defending the weak, and many other courses, has become pervasive at every stratum of the society the world over.

THE EVIL OF WITCHCRAFT

In the Bible, God hates witchcraft. In Deuteronomy 18: 10-12 (NKJV), it is written, "There shall not be found among you anyone who makes his son or his daughter pass through the fire, or one who practices witchcraft (divination), or a soothsayer (fortune teller), or one who interprets omens, or a sorcerer, or one who conjures spells (cast spells), or a medium, or a spiritist, or one who calls up the dead (necromancy). For all who do these things are an abomination to the LORD, and because of these abominations, the LORD has driven them out from before you." In Leviticus 20:27 God said, "A man or woman who is a medium or spiritist among you must be put to death. You are to stone them; their blood will be upon their own heads".

This means that if a witch is killed because of their witchcraft, they themselves are responsible and accountable for their death. Exodus 22:18 says, "You shall not permit a sorcerer to live." Another version says, "Thou shalt not suffer a witch to live." I believe God said that people should not allow a witch to live because of the spiritual wickedness of witchcraft and the evil that witches bring in people's lives.

The evils of witchcraft are demonstrated by the case of Balaam, the diviner who was hired for a good pay (handsome amount of money and benefits) by Balak, the king of Moab, who was the enemy of the children of Israel. Balaam was hired to curse the children of Israel and cause them to sin so they can lose the grace of God. Sin opens spiritual doors for evil attacks. Witchcraft works effectively where sin abides. Even Satan used witchcraft in a form of manipulation to cause Adam and Eve to sin and fall from the grace of God. Balak thrived on witchcraft to rule his nation. He needed the children of Israel to sin so he could overpower them in a physical war. This was a spiritual act of witchcraft and sorcery, which if successful, was going to render the children of Israel powerless and defeated in the physical battle. The impression here is that sin opens people to be bewitched and cursed. In return, those who are bewitched and cursed might think that their unpleasant experiences and sad outcomes are just life with its blows, never imagining that it is because they sinned and as a result became cursed and bewitched.

In the case of the children of Israel, because there was no iniquity or sin found in them, they could not be cursed and bewitched to misbehave. Balaam had to connive a way through divination and witchcraft to get the children of Israel to sin so he could perform what he was hired to do, i.e., to curse them. This gives the impression that in some cases, people misbehave because they are bewitched. Witchcraft can cause people to misbehave and in turn lose their blessings and suffer. The loss of blessings and sufferings are the goal.

For as long as the children of Israel obeyed God and did not sin, they could not be cursed. Witchcraft could not work on them. However, when sin entered, the sin of sexual immorality and eating food sacrificed to idols (ancestral/idol worship), curses could be laid upon them, and they suffered as a result (Numbers 22, 31).

Balaam and Balak, just like witches, were persistent in their evil desires and plans. Eventually, they succeeded. The children of Israel were not aware that some people were plotting their demise through divination, witchcraft, and sorcery. This reveals that for curses to work, there must be a sin in place. Also, it reveals that the sin in people can be engineered through witchcraft, divination, and sorcery. It is like a cycle. First, perform witchcraft that manipulates a person to sin, then unleash evil on them. Therefore, the thing to resist is the temptation to sin once a person is delivered, in order to overcome witchcraft and the plans of the enemy.

The children of Israel did not have the advantage born-again Christians have today to nullify the wickedness of Balaam and Balak. Today born-again Christians overcome the works of darkness by the blood of Jesus Christ and the name of Jesus Christ, as well as the Holy Spirit. The saving grace of God through Jesus Christ and his blood redeem people from curses and the consequences of sin. God forgives and cleanses from all unrighteousness those who confess their sins and repent from their ways. 1 John 1:9 (NKJV) says, "If we confess our sins, he is faithful and just to forgive us our sins and to cleanse us from all unrighteousness." When God forgives, he doesn't remember those forgiven sins. Those sins are washed away by the blood of Jesus and erased completely. Hebrews 8:12 (NIV) says, "For I will forgive their wickedness and will remember their sins no more." The new covenant through the blood of Jesus Christ gives the born-again Christians the privilege that God gave to the children of Israel in Jeremiah 31:34, namely, of having their sins forgiven and not remembered. Only Satan reminds people of their confessed sins to cast doubt whether the sins are forgiven or not.

This was the case even in the sin of Adam and Eve. The devil engineered the sin in them, and used disobedience, which the Bible says is as the sin of witchcraft. So, the devil caused Eve to doubt God's instructions not to eat from the tree of the knowledge of good and evil. The devil approached Eve and not Adam because Eve was not yet created when God gave Adam the instruction not to eat from that tree. So, it was easy for Eve to doubt, and their sin made them loose the grace of God and dominion on the earth, and caused them to die spiritually. Witchcraft caused Adam and Eve to sin and lose the grace of God. The devil then took away the dominion of the earth from Adam and Eve and became the god of this world until Jesus Christ came to redeem humanity from the powers of Satan, death, and hell. It is no surprise that those who practice witchcraft and sorcery will have their part in the lake of fire. Witchcraft was the first evil work of darkness on earth. Witchcraft practices are extremely evil, demonic, and satanic as they manipulate people to get them to do what they would otherwise not do.

Everything listed in the Bible that will cause people to experience the second death is all the works of the flesh, the level at which Satan, the evil spirits, and demons appeal to persuade and entice humans. The evil spirits work at the flesh level. In Galatians 5:19-21, it says, "The acts of the flesh are obvious: sexual immorality, impurity and debauchery, idolatry and witchcraft, hatred, discord, jealousy, fits of rage, selfish ambitions, dissensions, factions, and envy, drunkenness, orgies and the like. I warn you, as I did before, that those who live like this will not inherit the kingdom of God."

According to Galatians 5:16, the solution to the issue of the flesh is to walk in the Spirit, i.e., being filled and baptized in the Holy Spirit, and allowing the Holy Spirit to guide and lead you. It says, "Walk in the Spirit and you shall not fulfill the lust of the flesh." It is important to resist the temptations of the enemy and the flesh through prayer.

What makes life a mystery is that we are spirit beings clothed in mortal bodies. People are affected by everything around them because everything that God has created has life, hears God, and can even speak. Joshua 24:27 says, "Behold, this stone shall be a witness to us, for it has heard all the words of the LORD which He spoke to us." Creation does hear and speak to God, who created everything. Therefore, everything created by God has life and does speak to God because God is life. Even the blood and the ground (land) speak. It is written that the blood of Jesus Christ speaks better things than the blood of Abel (Hebrews 12:24).

Abel was the first person murdered on earth by his brother Cain. The blood of Abel was a witness and cried to God from the ground and God came and spoke to Cain, giving him his judgment. In Genesis 4:10-11, God said to Cain, "What have you done? The voice of your brother's blood is crying to Me from the ground. Now you are cursed from the ground, which has opened its mouth to receive your brother's blood from your hand."

The Bible says life is in the blood. In Leviticus 17:11 (NKJV), it is written, "For the life of the flesh is in the blood." This is true for born again Christians, who receive God's saving grace through the shed blood of Jesus Christ at the cross of Calvary. It is also true for non-Christians who sacrifice animals and other creatures/things at the evil altars to draw life and power from that blood. For the born-again Christians, the blood of Jesus Christ gives life and power, and nothing can ever oppose it in the hands and words of those who truly walk with Jesus Christ.

My people perish because of lack of knowledge (Hosea 4:6)

This Bible verse is very true of my life before I came to know and accepted Jesus Christ as my Lord and Savior.

THE EARLY YEARS OF MY LIFE

The Spiritual Realm And My Early Encounters With God

My journey to Jesus Christ testifies that Jesus Christ is the only way, the only truth, and the only life and that everything the Bible says is true.

It is a wonderful thing that when you are a child of God, Satan cannot have you for too long. When the Lord comes for you, Satan must let go because you were never his in the first place. In Galatians 4:1-7 (NKJV), it says, "Now I say that the heir, as long as he is a child, does not differ at all from a slave, though he is master (lord) of all, but is under guardians and stewards until the time appointed of the Father. Even so we, when we were children, were in bondage under the elements of the world. But when the fullness of the time had come, God sent forth His Son, born of a woman, born under the law, to redeem those who were under the law, that we might receive the adoption as sons. And because you are sons, God has sent forth the Spirit of His Son into your hearts, crying out, "Abba Father!." Therefore you are no longer a slave but a son, and if a son, then an heir of God though Christ." I believe the guardians and stewards here refer to parents, family, and people with positions of authority over our lives before becoming born-again children of God.

Jesus Christ said those whom God has given to him, he will not lose even one. In John 6:39, it says, "And this is the will of God, that I should not lose even one of all those he has given me, but that I should raise them up at the last day." I believe these are the last days we are living in, and Jesus Christ has woken me up from spiritual slumber. I was lost and Jesus Christ found me. Now I am happy that I am a child of God and certain about it.

1. Church Exposure before coming to Christ

It was at a very young age when I became aware of the existence of God. I think it was an innate knowledge I always had in my heart and mind. As a child, I felt very close to God, felt his presence all the time, loved him dearly and would always say "when I leave this earth, I want to go back to God. This world is too evil." I felt like I came from God and would one day go back to him.

Raised in a religious home by loving and caring parents, my family belonged to the Anglican Church. I was religious because even though I knew and believed that God exists, church customs and traditions shaped my "Christian" life and understanding, rather than the Word of God, Jesus Christ, and the Spirit of God. I did not know Jesus Christ who is the Word of God. I did not know I needed to have Jesus Christ in order to fulfil my desire to go back to God at the end of my days on earth. I certainly did not know him as my personal Lord and Savior for many years though I called myself a Christian. I was told He was the Son of God and did not understand how He alone was the Son of God. I thought Jesus Christ was selfish to call himself the Son of God and it was unfair for people to say he was the Son of God.

I used to be so bothered by this and felt rejected because only Jesus Christ was said to be the child of God. I felt I too was a child of God. I was secretly quite jealous of Jesus' position as the Son of God. I had no idea that because of Him and through Him, I too can become a child of God when I confess and accept him as my Lord and Savior and put my hope and trust in him.

The church I grew up attending did not introduce and present Jesus Christ well to me as a young person. There were just so many things I did not know and understand about him until I came to know him in my adulthood. They told us, in the Apostles' Creed and Nicene Creed that Jesus Christ is God in flesh who became a human being so he can die and raise again to forgive us our sins. I recited these creeds without understanding what I was saying and what it meant. They were just nice words. I did not understand how God can become a person. I guess many people did not really understand this. I even heard some people around me saying He was the ancestor of the Jewish people, and I thought they were right and believed them. This made me think that any person that dies becomes an ancestor of those who are related to them and are still alive, connecting the living to God and mediating in heaven on their behalf. This was a big lie of the devil which many around the world who reject Jesus Christ believe. I thought dead people had a meaning to the living. I trust that unbelief, practices of darkness and myriads of religious beliefs the world over are rooted in these kinds of ideologies.

Poor presentation of Jesus Christ by churches proclaiming to be Christians, especially in Sunday schools, during teenage years (Confirmation) and the use of extra biblical books like the catechism and the Book of Common Prayer do play a role in confusing the masses. These books are not the Bible and should not be treated as such. They are not the pure, infallible Word of God that transforms and make a way of salvation through Christ. I also believe these books dilute the message of the Bible and can easily cause people to go astray and reject the Gospel and the need to be born again. Those books give you enough to fool you that you are a Christian and do not need a Savior and little to keep you deceived that you are going to heaven after death because you submitted to church customs and traditions. I call them an orchestrated deception, a plan of the devil using pseudo, half-baked truth in the church to lead people astray. These are the books my church used the most growing up to conduct church services. They are religious books.

The Bible says how can they believe if they do not hear, and how can they hear without a preacher? In Romans 10:13-14 (NLT), it says, "Everyone who calls on the name of the LORD will be saved. But how can they call on him to save them unless they believe in him? And how can they believe in him if they have never heard about him? And how can they hear about him unless someone tells them?."

This is the reason Jesus Christ told us to go into the ends of the world and make disciples and baptize them in the name of the Father, the Son and the Holy Spirit (Matthew 28:19-20). In Mark 16:15-16, Jesus Christ said, "Go into the world and preach the gospel to all creation. Whoever believes and is baptized shall be saved, but whoever does not believe will be condemned."

In the Anglican church that I attended, I do not ever recall hearing that people needed a Savior and needed to be saved. I don't recall any altar call inviting the lost to give their lives to Christ. There was no preacher who spoke about that. They followed a structured, well-planned program in every service. Whatever we chanted using the church books and the creeds never made it into my heart to transform me or convict me of sin because that's not their purpose. I believe their purpose is to inculcate submission to the customs, practices, and traditions of the church. Only the word of God, written in the Bible, can transform people, expose sin and the need for salvation through Christ Jesus.

Growing up, as religious people, I and many around me, were not born again and were generally skeptical of born-again Christians. There was a tendency to make fun of and mock the born-again Christians. The born-again Christians were normally referred to as "the Jesus people" and perceived to be fanatics, docile, and boring. This was bullying. It was of the devil, wanting to instill shame to those who followed the true path. They were looked down upon and considered backward. I recall the comment when someone became a better person than they normally were or performed a great act of kindness, people would usually ask mockingly if they had found Jesus. People also thought it was only those who were desperate for marriage or those to whom life has dealt a blow who became born-again Christians. Being born again was seen as an escape cocoon for the weak and cowards. To fit in socially, no one wanted to be labelled a Jesus person. As a result, there were hardly any born-again Christians around me in my youth. If there were any, they did a good job of hiding themselves.

My Christian life as a young girl was barely there. I went to church, was taught to be a good person, enjoyed singing hymns, prayed for food and travels, sometimes at bedtime, and read church literature but not the Bible. To me, this was Christianity and the best way to serve God and get to heaven. I do not recall reading the Bible growing up. I knew very little about what the Bible said about many things. I did not know that the Bible said everything about everything meaningful to living a successful life here on earth. I think the Bible provides the **B**est **I**nstructions **B**efore **L**iving **E**arth to anyone who care about life here and after. It gives clear requirements to meet in or for the Kingdom of God to come and His will be done in a person's life on earth and in heaven.

Over time, as we grew up into our teenage and young adulthood, all the religious practices at home became weaker and weaker until they almost all disappeared. It's impossible and unsustainable to keep religion or keep up with it because it does not allow the only reliable, dependable, and powerful human helper, who is the Holy Spirit, to get involved. What remained for me was only sporadic church attendance and infrequent prayer until I moved away from home to go to university. The main prayer that remained the longest for the family was the prayer for travel mercies whenever anyone was travelling long distances. At some point, we even stopped saying the grace before meals. The two things that I am grateful I have learned from school assembly are the Lord's Prayer and Psalm 23. Every student, whether Christian or non-Christian, was expected to memorize and recite frequently the Lord's Prayer and Psalm 23 (and sometimes Psalm 24). These came in handy later in life when I faced challenges and needed to pray and did not know what to say.

2. Unbiblical Church Practices

Church baptism: Our church, being a religious institution, "baptized" me and many others as infants by pouring and sprinkling water on the head. I do not actually know the exact age I got baptized. From what I saw, infants as young as six months got baptized and it was a big party when that happened. I think adults used child Christening and baptismal as an excuse to eat good food and drink. Honestly, what did I know about sin and baptism as an infant? The sprinkling of church water on a little child's head does not even come close to the baptism written about in the Bible and certainly does not free those children from generational curses caused by the sins, transgressions, and iniquities of their families and parents.

Christian Baptism: Christian baptism by immersion in the water is the only biblical baptism instructed by Jesus Christ. It is written nowhere in the Bible that any one and certainly not any church should baptize children and infants. Instead, baptism comes after believing that Jesus Christ is the Son of God who came in the flesh to save the world from sin. A person needs to confess and repent, ask for forgiveness for their personal sin, call on the name of Jesus Christ, and ask to be saved. This tells us that a person needs to be of age where they can personally understand their need for a Savior and believe because salvation is personal. This is demonstrated in Acts 8:26-40 (KJV), where the Spirit of the Lord instructed Phillip to join the Ethiopian eunuch who was reading from the book of Isaiah about Jesus Christ but did not understand it.

It says in verse 35-39 "Then Phillip opened his mouth, and began at the same scripture, and preached unto him Jesus. And as they went on their way, they came unto certain water: and the eunuch said, See, here is water, what doth hinder me to be baptized? And Phillip said, if thou believest with all thine heart, thou mayest. And he answered and said, I believe that Jesus Christ is the Son of God. And he commanded the chariot to stand still: and they went down both into water, both Phillip and the eunuch; and he baptized him. And when they were come up out of the water, the Spirit of the Lord caught away Phillip, that the eunuch saw him no more; and went on his way rejoicing."

The eunuch believed because he was grown up, able to hear the preaching of Phillip, and discern that what Phillip was preaching was true. He was then baptized, dying with Christ by immersion in water and rising again with Christ when he came out of the water. This is the only water baptism that the Bible commands. He was a new creation in Christ.

Jesus Christ was baptized by John in the Jordan River by immersion when he was of age. Given this, I believe if Christianity is to follow Christ, then Christians need to do what He did.

In John 3:5, Jesus said, "Truly, truly I say to you, unless one is born of water and the Spirit, he cannot enter the kingdom of God."

In Romans 6:3-4, it says, "Do you know that all of us who have been baptized into Christ Jesus were baptized into his death? We were buried therefore with him by baptism into death, in order that, just as Christ was raised from the dead by the glory of the Father, we too might walk in newness of life."

In Acts 2:38, Peter said, "Repent and be baptized every one of you in the name of Jesus Christ for the forgiveness of your sins, and you will receive the gift of the Holy Spirit." Here Peter was not talking to infants and children. He was talking to grown-ups who understood what it is to sin, repent, and be forgiven of sin.

In Matthew 3:11, John said, "I baptize you with water for repentance, but he who is coming after me is mightier than I, whose sandals I am not worthy to carry. He will baptize you with the Holy Spirit and fire."

In Matthew 28:19-20, Jesus Christ commanded the disciples, saying, "Go therefore and make disciples of all nations, baptizing them in the name of the Father, and of the Son and of the Holy Spirit, teaching them to observe all that I have commanded you. And behold, I am with you always, to the end of the age." You cannot make a disciple out of an infant.

3. Misconceptions About Christianity And Salvation

The belief and faith of parents never saves their children. Before baptism, the Bible requires you to confess your sins, repent, and accept Jesus Christ as your personal Lord and Savior. How can a child who is yet to speak do that? They do not know they are sinners and need a Savior. Whatever the spiritual meaning of that infant and child baptism is, only the church knows. This is unbiblical whether performed at an Anglican or any other church. According to the scriptures, Christians must confess their sins and confess Jesus Christ as their personal Lord and Savior, believe in their heart that God raised him up from the dead (Romans 10:9), be born again by grace through faith in the finished work of the Jesus Christ at the Cross of Calvary and by the Spirit of the living God before they can be baptized. At this stage, a person receives the gift of salvation. It is a gift because it is God's grace to humanity, received freely by those who are wise enough to believe.

With my knowledge and understanding of the Bible today, child baptism is unbiblical and a religious practice. It is not Christianity. I wonder why the church practices and observes infant/toddler baptism even to this day. When John baptized people, he asked them to bring fruit worthy of repentance, implying that those who came to his baptismal were people who knew and understood right from wrong, of a responsible age and accountable for their actions.

Even Jesus Christ went to the temple at the age of twelve where he spoke to the teachers of the law about the scriptures and was baptized by John when he was an adult. Jesus Christ had no sin to confess and therefore needed no repentance. He was baptized to fulfil the scriptures and show us the way.

There is just no evidence of child baptismal in the Bible. Infants and toddlers cannot be immersed in water; they will drown. They have no knowledge of sin or any sin to confess. They are not even aware of their parents' and family's sins. I wonder if the church does this on purpose so many people can grow up trapped in religion, deceived and headed to a destructive end in hell at the end of their lives. Living and growing up as a religious person, destruction and hopelessness in life here on earth and afterwards are inevitable. But the merciful God shows compassion and mercy, revealing the truth by His Word and His Spirit.

Christian baptism by immersion in the water symbolizes that we died with Christ, and we are risen with him. It is at this stage of the new birth that the heart of a believer gets circumcised and is filled with the Holy Spirit. While water baptism is performed by human beings outwardly, it is a powerful spiritual act separating born-again Christians from other kinds of Christians. A born-again Christian get baptized twice, first by water through human hands and then by Holy Spirit's fire. It is the second baptism that give Christians a victorious life whether rich or poor, Jew or Gentile, black or white.

The baptism of the Holy Spirit and fire is, however, only received spiritually, inwardly from Jesus Christ himself. No human being can give another person the Holy Spirit. He comes from the Father in heaven. Humans can lay hands and pray for another to be baptized in the Holy Spirit, and it is Jesus Christ who sends Him as He answers that prayer. The baptismal of the Holy Spirit and fire empowers born-again Christians to perform many bold things (miracles and wonders) with confidence, such as preaching, delivering and healing people, prophesying, challenging the forces of darkness without fear, offering prayers that can change the course of things, and many other things. This empowerment is critical for a born-again Christian to live a victorious life. The Apostles were told to wait for this baptism before they went out boldly to proclaim Jesus Christ as the Savior of the world, performing great signs and wonders.

The Holy Spirit is a very active help in people becoming born again, as we have seen in the case of the Eunuch and Phillip. When a person gets born again, the Holy Spirit comes in them immediately to dwell. They receive the Holy Spirit but are not filled with the Holy Spirit. They still need the baptism of the Holy Spirit and fire. This Spirit and fire baptism come in various ways.

A person can pray and ask for it or the hands of those that are already baptized in the Holy Spirit and fire, can be laid on them through prayer to receive the baptism. In the case of the Apostles, the Holy Spirit and fire came when they were praying and waiting in the upper room in Jerusalem as instructed by Jesus Christ. It is important to bear in mind that before Jesus Christ was crucified, he washed the Apostles' feet and saying to Peter, he may not understand what he was doing but later he would (John13:7). I believe the washing of the disciples' feet was important to prepare them for the baptism of the Holy Spirit and fire.

After seeing Jesus Christ ascend into heaven 40 days after he was with the Apostles after the resurrection, Acts 1:12-14 and Acts 2:1-4 say, "Then they (Apostles) returned to Jerusalem from the Mount of Olives, which is near the city, a Sabbath day's journey away. When they arrived, they went to the upper room where they were staying. With one accord, they all continued in prayer, along with the women and Mary the mother of Jesus and His brothers." "When the day of Pentecost came, they were all together in one place.

Suddenly a sound like a mighty rushing wind came from heaven and filled the whole house where they were sitting. They saw tongues like flames of fire that separated and came to rest on each of them. And they were all filled with the Holy Spirit and began to speak in other tongues as the Spirit enabled them."

In the case of believers in Ephesus, it says in Acts 19:1-3 (NLT), "While Apollos was in Corinth, Paul traveled through the interior regions until he reached Ephesus, on the coast, where he found believers. 'Did you receive the Holy Spirit when you believed?', he asked them. 'No, they replied, we haven't even heard that there is a Holy Spirit'. So Paul asked, 'Then what baptism did you experience?' he asked. And they replied, 'The baptism of John'. Paul said "John's baptism called for repentance from sin. But John himself told the people to believe in the one who would come later, meaning Jesus'. As soon as they heard this, they were baptized in the name of the Lord Jesus. Then when Paul laid his hands on them, the Holy Spirit came on them, and they spoke in other tongues and prophesied."

I have observed that only born-again Christians, who believe that the Holy Spirit is still working in the children of God, would normally receive the baptism of the Holy Spirit and fire that only Jesus Christ can give. This is a spiritual baptism, evidenced by speaking in tongues, the ability to resist sin, and live a wholesome, abundant Christian life. As Jesus Christ says in Mark 16:17 (NKJV), "And these signs will follow those who believe: In my name they will cast out demons, they will speak in new tongues; they will take up serpents; and if they drink anything deadly, it will by no means hurt them; they will lay hands on the sick and they will recover". This explains why I have never seen signs and wonders, the working of the Holy Spirit in the Anglican Church that I attended growing up.

Since I became a born-again Christian, I have observed that those Christians and churches that deny the working of the Holy Spirit, such as Baptist and Reformed churches, typically do not receive the baptism of the Holy Spirit and fire. Therefore, their congregants do not really know the power of the name Jesus Christ. I have come to realize that to be an effective Christian, pray, and see powerful results with people being healed, delivered, evangelized effectively, taught with power, and live as Christ calls Christians to live, a Christian needs the baptism of the Holy Spirit and fire from Jesus Christ.

I recall two Baptist churches I used to attend. When I told them about deliverance and that the Lord told me I needed deliverance, one said that it is of the devil and the other said it was African witchcraft. The Holy Spirit did not hesitate to tell me I should come out of Baptist church and told me the kind of a church to look for. I am grateful I listened and obeyed the voice of the Holy Spirit. I truly needed to be delivered from many things as a born-again Christian. My deliverance was not even a one-time event, it was a process over a few years. Throughout the process, I came to learn many things about the spirit realms and the power of the name of Jesus Christ.

Christians are supernaturally empowered with the Holy Spirit and fire by Jesus Christ. They need this empowerment not to be overcome by evil. As a Christian, a person becomes an enemy of Satan and darkness, and faces spiritual experiences and warfare that only the Holy Spirit and the fire of Jesus Christ can help them deal with. Therefore, whatever they do, they do in the name of Jesus Christ. My religious Anglican church never taught me this or demonstrated the power.

Prayer and the religious spirit: When I was in a religious church, I thought the Father and the Son were separate, individual persons, and the Holy Spirit was not a person but an "it." I thought of them as human beings like me and not as Spirit. Honestly, I never understood the meaning behind the church's practices, traditions, and customs. In my childlike mind, those customs were Christianity and very confusing. I thought all I needed to have God's favor and enter heaven was to be a good person and do all I can in my strength to live a holy life. I failed miserably trying to be holy by my strength and good works. I do not know anyone who has ever succeeded. I knew nothing about the grace of God because I did not know or understand the scriptures.

Whenever prayer was offered, I do not recall it being offered in the name of Jesus Christ. I knew that there was the Father, the Son and the Holy Spirit as my church tradition was to offer prayer in the name of the Father, the Son and the Holy Spirit and motioned it in a gesture of the cross at the end of prayer. Other than this, I never understood what it meant.

The Bible says that we should always offer prayer in the name of Jesus Christ for God to harken unto our prayers and for Jesus Christ to answer the Christian prayer. Following the church customs and traditions, I offered prayer in the name of the Father, the Son and the Holy Spirit, motioning with my hand the sign of the cross. So, not having a clue what the Bible says about prayer, I felt somewhat holy and spiritual each time I portrayed the symbol of the cross at the end of my prayer. I think the gesture of the cross is basically saying that prayer is offered in the name of the cross and crucifixion and not in the name of the risen King and the only name given to true Christians by God to call and use in prayer.

There is nowhere in the Bible where it says pray in the name of the Father. It says pray to the Father in the name of Jesus Christ. Nowhere in the Bible does it say pray in the name of Holy Spirit or the Son. It is not biblical for Christians to pray in the name of the Father, the Son and the Holy Spirit and portray this reverence in a gesture of the cross. There is of course a place in the Bible where it says baptize in the name of the Father, and of the Son and of the Holy Spirit (Matthew28:19).

The Bible categorically and clearly states that we should pray only in the name of Jesus Christ. It says in Acts 4:11- (NKJV) that "This is the stone, which was rejected by you builders, which has become the chief cornerstone."

However, each time I did the cross gesture, it made me feel like a proud "Christian." This was so ingrained in me such that after learning that prayer to God must only be offered in the name of Jesus Christ, I battled to get rid of the cross gesture at the end of my prayer. It was a real spiritual battle. I felt like the name of Jesus Christ alone was not enough. It needed help, and I needed to seal it with the cross gesture. It took me a long time to drop the cross gesture at the end of prayer, even after becoming a believer. I would say "in Jesus' name" but proceed to say "in the name of the Father, the son and the Holy Spirit," portraying the cross afterwards. It felt like the prayer was not complete by only saying "in Jesus' name."

This was clearly a lie from the pit of hell, nullifying prayers of the ignorant. It makes the name of Jesus Christ weak in the mind of people and that we are righteous in ourselves to approach God. This is how much religion can indoctrinate people. These are the little things that people may not realize when it comes to the unbiblical impact of religion and its practices and how much religious institutions can hold someone's mind hostage due to institutionalized customs and traditions. Religion is not Christianity. Religion has a lot of man-made supplements and alternatives to the Bible and what God and Jesus Christ command.

It took a lot of spiritual, demonic attacks where I just called the name of Jesus Christ and saw demons, witches and Satan flee that I came to realize that the name of Jesus Christ alone is more than enough to defeat the powers of darkness.

Jesus Christ is the name that allows born-again Christians to approach God the Father and to receive the holy Spirit and have power to challenge darkness. Only the name of Jesus Christ is above all names in the physical and the spirit realm. There are multiple Bible verses that tell us to pray and ask in the name of Jesus Christ, and that it is the only name that can save human beings.

In Acts 4:12, it says, "And there is salvation in no one else, for there is no other name under heaven that has been given among men by which we must be saved." In John 14:3 and 6, Jesus Christ says, "Whatever you ask in my name, that will I do, so that the Father may be glorified in the Son" and "I am the way, the truth and the life and no one comes to the Father but through me."

In Colossians 3:17, it says, "Whatever you do in word or deed, do all in the name of the Lord Jesus, giving thanks through him to God the Father." In John 14:14, Jesus Christ said, "If you ask me anything in my name, I will do it." And in John 15:16, he said, "You did not choose me, but I chose you, and appointed you that you would go and bear fruit, and that your fruit would remain, so that whatever you ask of the Father in my name, He may give to you."

All these verses reveal that following the church customs and tradition without understanding the scriptures is like the blind leading the blind, and both will fall into a ditch. It can lead a person to hell. In the spirit realm, ignorance is not an excuse. A religious church or teacher and their ideologies can really cost people eternity with Christ. Religious ignorance can take a person to hell.

The religious spirit is a very strong spirit, and I believe it is the spirit of Satan that wants people not to know the truth and the power of the name of Jesus Christ, which is more than enough for those who believe in Jesus Christ. Half-truth is dangerous. There are a lot of unbelieving "Christians," whom I have come to call "church goers" instead of born-again Christians. I believe anyone who does not offer prayer in the name of Jesus Christ is basically offering in their own name which is blasphemous to God because without Jesus Christ, no one can approach God. We are all unrighteous to approach God. Only the name of Jesus Christ and his blood that washes believers clean give believers the grace to approach God.

I am now free of that spirit and only pray according to what the Bible says and commands, to pray only in the name of Jesus Christ. In John 14:13-14 and 16:23-24 (NKJV), Jesus Christ says, "And whatever you ask in My name, that I will do, that the Father may be glorified in the Son. If you ask anything in My name, I will do it. And in that day, you will ask Me nothing. Most assuredly, I say to you, whatever you ask the Father in My name, He will give you. Until now you have asked nothing in My name. Ask and you will receive, that your joy may be full."

The only time the Bible says Christian should do something in the name of the Father, and of the Son and of the Holy Spirit is with regards to water baptism by immersion in the water as Jesus Christ has commanded (Matthew 28:19-20 NKJV). I believe only truly born-again Christians are qualified to baptize people. People can also be baptized only in the name of Jesus as stated in Acts 19:5 (NLT) that says, "As soon as they heard this, they were baptized in the name of the Lord Jesus."

Religious Pride: Growing up, there was a sense of religious pride in our religiosity and "churchianity," which tended to make us look down upon those who were born-again Christians. They were regarded as fanatics, extreme, and strange. We thought we were the only true Christians and did not know we were the ones who were in darkness, without the saving grace of God and headed to hell. The arrogance and foolishness of this kind of attitude is expounded beautifully in Isaiah

5:20 (NKJV) that says, "Woe to those who call evil good and good evil; who put darkness for light and light for darkness, who put bitter for sweet and sweet for bitter."

The born-again Christians were the light that we failed to recognize, just like those who failed to recognize Jesus Christ when he walked the face of the earth and ended up crucifying him. They were also consumed by religious pride and failed to recognize the Savior of their souls. I am convinced many people alive today would have shouted "crucify him" were they there when He was crucified. In John 1:5 (NKJV), it says, "And the light shines in the darkness and the darkness did not comprehend it." We were in darkness with our religiosity. The darkness was considered normal life. It dealt me and many others many blows that only the light that comes as the result of new birth in Christ can cast away.

Religious pride is dangerous, surely not of God and is the result of the fruit of the flesh. True Christians can never be proud of what God has given to them so freely. Instead, a true Christian is humbled and grateful for what they have received through salvation that is only found in Christ Jesus. A true Christian gets burdened by the spiritual disposition and conditions of others and wants everyone to know what they know and have what they have. A true Christian wants everyone to be saved and be free from spiritual oppression, possession, slumber, and blindness. They have a heart to go out into the world and make disciples for the kingdom of God in various ways. They have the heart for the lost souls blindly roaming the earth. They would go to the ends of the world, to remote jungles to preach the word of God and make disciples.

The marks of a true Christian are detailed in Matthew 5-7 by Jesus Christ in the Sermon on the Mount. Repentance of sin and dependence on Jesus Christ, His name, His blood, and His power by His Spirit are also marks of a true Christian. Now that I know about the spirit realm from the Biblical perspective and personal experiences, I can confidently conclude that religious and spiritual pride are certainly the works of demons hiding in people and institutions of worship.

In Job 41, it says leviathan is the king over all that are proud. It says in Job 41:33-34 (NKJV), "On earth there is nothing like him, which is made without fear. He beholds every high (proud) thing; He is the king over all the children of pride." It is this same spirit that hardens people's hearts and causes them to reject the gospel because of pride. In Job 41:24, it says, "His (leviathan's) heart is as hard as stone, even as hard as the lower millstone." It is an anti-Christ spirit, scared of being discovered and cast out once people are born again. It gives people a religious spirit. Once the person is truly born again, pride and heart-hardness have no place as the Holy Spirit, who is meek and gentle, comes into the hearts of believers, destroying all the nature and characteristics of leviathan. This leviathan spirit work tirelessly in the hearts of many who refuse and reject the gospel. I believe it is this spirit that is responsible for diverse religions of this world that reject Jesus Christ as the only begotten son of God and as God. I believe it is also behind pseudo-Christianity.

The fruit of the Holy Spirit in Galatians 5:22-23, which is love, joy, peace, patience, kindness, goodness, faithfulness, gentleness/meekness, and self-control, casts away all the leviathan's nature in born-again Christians as the Holy Spirit comes to abide in them.

I believe religious pride is fueled by the anti-Christ spirit which blinds the people from coming into the true knowledge of the Bible and their inheritance in God, Jesus Christ, and the Holy Spirit. This spirit is also responsible for making people commit the sin of unbelief and idolatry, worshipping other things, ungodly deities who are basically Satan and demons and false gods, which are abomination to the true, living God.

God says that "My people perish because of lack of knowledge" (Hosea 4:6) and "Through knowledge shall the just be delivered" (Proverbs 11:9). The knowledge of the gospel and believing the gospel of Jesus Christ bring the light of God into the lives of people and set the captives free. Believing the gospel turns people from being the children of the night and darkness into the children of day and light. 1

Thessalonians 5:5 (NIV) says, "You are all children of the light and children of the day. We do not belong to the night or to the darkness."

It is not in the interest of the evil spirits that anyone should know the truth, the way, and the life in Christ. They work overtime to keep people in darkness. Spiritual blindness is real, and many suffer from it. Imagine the number of religions the demons and Satan have established in the world that are so different from each other but serve the same master to deceive the people throughout the world and generations. The world is full of a buffet of spiritual practices that worship the same spirit unknowingly. Each group think they are on the right path and unique while they are not. This is even happening in the Christian circles. There are false churches and cults (pseudo-Christians) posing as Christian churches. Some even think that they are the illuminated ones through their beliefs, ideologies, traditions, customs, and practices when they are really in darkness. In Isaiah 5:21 and 24 (NKJV), it says, "Woe to those who are wise in their own eyes, and prudent (clever) in their own sight. Because they have rejected the law of the LORD of hosts and despised the word of the Holy One of Israel."

Religion without Christ and Salvation equals blindness: Most people in my place of birth were just religious churchgoers who did not live according to the word and the Spirit of God. The system was very confusing and precarious. A very dangerous setup, spiritually and physically. People would go to church and afterwards go and do whatever suited their flesh, including visiting spiritists and witchdoctors, getting drunk, and committing sins of all kinds. Even the people in church leadership did that. I guess people did this to fill the gap in their lives that only Jesus Christ and the Holy Spirit can fill. People wanted problems solved and had to look outside the church for solutions because the church had none to offer. It was works-based religiosity.

The Anglican church had no message of repentance and salvation and therefore many were in a state of vulnerability, emptiness, and ignorance when it came to living a spirit filled Christian life.

With regards to alcohol drinking, I had observed that most people started drinking alcohol once they started taking the holy communion at church. The reason I believe this happened is because the church served real alcohol to those who were confirmed by the church and were therefore qualified to take the holy communion, typically at age 16 after completing the year-long confirmation class. This initiation was strategically done in the final year of high school, when many would be leaving the safety of their parents as they move on to higher institutions. I believe this desensitized people, especially the youth, to alcohol drinking. Some will even say Jesus turned water into wine to justify their drinking problem. The church had a few alcoholics, even among the deacons.

As church people, like many other people in the world, we broke all the Ten Commandments. We were not diligent in keeping the commandments of God. We heard them but did not conceive them in our heart, spirit, and soul. We did not have the Holy Spirit as our advocate and helper, who helps born-again Christians from stumbling and protects them from the tricks of the enemy. In fact, it was impossible to have the Holy Spirit living in any of us because we were not saved, did not believe and confess that Jesus Christ is our Lord and Savior, and were not baptized by immersion in the water. There was no relationship with Christ Jesus who baptizes believers with the Holy Spirit and fire. Jesus Christ sends the Holy Spirit into the hearts of believers at the point of conversion to help Christians in their walk here on earth. Although I knew about the Holy Trinity, I did not understand that the Holy Spirit was also a person. Truly, as the Bible says in Proverbs 11:9 (KJV), "An hypocrite with his mouth destroyeth his neighbor; but through knowledge shall the just be delivered."

When I had religion without Christ and his saving grace, I had an idea that a Christian must live a holy life. However, I did not really understand what it meant to be a Christian living a holy life in the fallen world and what and how holy living entailed and looked like. Truly, God has written his laws in everyone's heart, which is why I knew I had to be holy, and even an unbeliever still knows right from wrong, moral from immoral.

The written law of God in my heart and parental teachings and guidance were what guided my heart on moral issues and distinguishing right from wrong. Without the knowledge and the teachings of the Bible, maneuvering life as a Christian becomes a losing battle. We are always surrounded by sin, spiritual experiences and unseen entities at every level. The more people sin, the more they become susceptible to sin. Unclean spirits are mostly instigators of and responsible for sinful life in people, even though people have free will to choose. Christians are not immune to the influences of their environments. They still go through unpleasant experiences. This is why it says in 1 Peter 5:8 (NKJV), "be sober, be vigilant, because your adversary the devil walks about like a roaring lion, seeking whom he may devour."

For a Christian not to be devoured by the devil, it says in James 4:7 (KJV), "Submit yourselves therefore to God. Resist the devil, and he will flee from you." The first thing a Christian must evaluate and assess is whether they are submitted to God or how much are they submitting daily. Without submitting to God, a Christian can become an easy prey for the devil and his evil minions. A Christian needs to stay submitted to Christ daily to overcome the schemes of the devil in the spirit and the physical realm. Romans 8:1 (NKJV) says, "There is therefore now no condemnation to those who are in Christ Jesus, who do not walk according to the flesh, but according to the Spirit." The Holy Spirit is the greatest helper every born-again Christian needs daily to stay submitted to God.

Easter: This was another unbiblical experience. Growing up, the Easter season and the church Easter customs and practices stood out for me. The Easter service was truly unique and felt very spiritual.

I liked the Easter service, especially the early morning (3am-6am) candlelight procession from the church to the graveyard, with the priests and deacons wearing their church robes, everyone holding a candle, singing hymns until the procession reached the graveyard. The singing was beautiful with everyone singing in unison. The sight was beautiful to behold and felt spiritual.

The church did this every year. It was an important custom that the Anglican church was known for. This procession attracted a lot of people in the town. I think this practice was to emulate the experiences of the women who went to Jesus' tomb early on the morning of Sunday after the Friday crucifixion. As part of the church custom, congregants were encouraged to remember and honor their dead relatives during Easter. I am not sure what was the purpose of mixing the resurrection of Jesus Christ with remembering and honoring dead relatives.

The Easter service was so popular and attracted even those who lived hours away from the town. People would travel home to attend this service. Some people only attended church once a year for the Easter service. To me, this was a sort of a pilgrimage for spiritual connection available once a year. Every Easter Sunday, the church would be full to the brim. It was a moving service that felt like I was there when Jesus was crucified and rose again. It felt very present. There was just something about that service that made it feel special in my heart, and I guess in the hearts of others.

Preparations for the Easter weekend were another experience and felt quite spiritual. A few weeks before Easter Sunday, church members went to clean up the graves of their dead relatives.

The Saturday before the Sunday resurrection of Christ, families would prepare garlands for each grave the family has, using a specific type of weed and leaves that had a unique smell. Once the garlands were prepared, they would put live flowers on the garlands, then soak them in the water until the 3 am church procession to the graveyard. The garlands would then be put on the graves of the loved ones on the early morning of the resurrection Sunday.

At 3 am, those who were able to get to the church would go there to start the processions with the priests and deacons. Once or twice, we were able to start the procession from the church.

Otherwise, each year we would wait to join them when they got closer to our neighborhood. We lived on one of the streets that led to the graveyard. So, it made sense to join when they got closer to our home.

Once the procession reached the graveyard, the priest would pick the grave of one of the deceased church members for the congregants to congregate around and conduct a church service there. The whole congregation would gather around the chosen grave for the service. I do not know what criteria they used to choose the grave of the deceased church member to visit. I assumed it was that of a dead prominent member of the church.

Once the service was ended, the congregation would be given about an hour to visit their family graves and place their highly decorated garlands on those graves. Some people spoke to the graves and their dead relatives, connecting spiritually with the unclean spirits of the dead and the graves. I thought going to the graves during Easter was what God required for people to remember Jesus Christ's death and resurrection. I thought every dead person who went to church was with God in heaven, and these church processions and practices pleased God.

At this stage, I did not know what the word of God commanded regarding the dead. As a result, I thought it was perfectly right for "Christians" to visit the graves and speak to their dead relatives because the Anglican church promoted this.

Holding church services at the graveyard and allowing congregants to embrace and talk at the graves of their dead relatives is completely unbiblical. It was the most spiritually misleading thing I have ever encountered at church. It gave the impression that somehow, the dead are still connected to the living. Before I started reading the Bible for myself, I thought the dead, whether they lived godly or ungodly, mediated for the living before God in heaven. I thought that after dying, people were all in heaven and served as spiritual communication links between the living and God. At this stage, I never gave much thought to the idea that some people go to hell and others go to heaven depending on whether they had accepted Christ and lived a righteous life or rejected him and lived unrighteously.

There is no place in the Bible where people are asked to visit the graves of their deceased or seek communication with them. Talking to the dead is necromancy. The Bible forbids such connections as indicated in Leviticus 20:27, which says, "A man or a woman who is a medium or a necromancer shall surely be put to death. They shall be stoned with stone; their blood shall be upon them."

Deuteronomy 18:9-14 outlines abominable practices before the LORD. Necromancy is one of those abominable practices before the LORD. It defiles the children of God. Nations were judged because of such abominable practices. Moses said to the children of Israel that "When you come into the land that the LORD your God is giving you, you shall not learn to follow the abominable practices of those nations. There shall not be found among you a necromancer or one who inquires of the dead, for whoever does these things is an abomination to the LORD."

Ecclesiastes 12:7 says, "And the dust returns to the earth as it was, and the spirit returns to God who gave it." Psalm 146:4 says, "When his breath departs, he returns to the earth, on that very day his plans perish."

It means that the dead people are dead, have no life in them and cannot do anything. Meaning when people die, it is the end of their connection to the living. Therefore, they cannot speak to the living or help the living in any way, shape, size, or form unless through the services of a necromancer. Those who practice necromancy violate the laws of the spirit as they do things that God forbids. They are an abomination to the LORD. It makes you wonder why a church would approve such a thing.

The witches who are necromancers can communicate with the dead people. In 1 Samuel 28, Saul, the first king of Israel, when God rejected him and did not answer his prayers through dreams or a prophet, he got so frustrated that he decided to visit a necromancer, the witch of Endor, so she could help him access Samuel from the place of the dead. This witch used her ritual pit to conjure up the spirit of Samuel from the dead. She called up Samuel the prophet through demonic powers from his resting place. Samuel came and rebuked Saul for disturbing him.

Samuel told Saul that the next day Saul and his sons would be killed, and it came to pass. Though the spirit of the person goes to God when they die, through witchcraft manipulation the dead can still be tempered with. Saul knew that the anointing of Samuel remained with Samuel even though Samuel had died. I think these kinds of practices must have been common during the times of Saul and kings who were not with God, engaged in such practices for guidance, protection and power. I believe this is still the case today for those who are not with the true living God.

Job 7:9-10 says, "As the cloud fades and vanishes, so he who goes down to Sheol does not come up, he returns no more to his house, nor does his place know him anymore." It indicates that any experiences of engaging with any deceased person, is of the devil. Those who appear as people's deceased relatives to give them instructions, power, talk to them or do anything for the living are familiar spirits, masquerading as their deceased relatives. Familiar spirits are evil spirits, demons that are familiar with a person's lineage, as they have been with families for generations.

Visits to gravesides are dangerous because they can connect the living to strange, unclean spirits of the grave. The same goes for practices of ancestral worship to connect to dead relatives or visiting spirit mediums. They connect people to familiar spirits and open them up to their possession and influence. These spirits can demand undivided worship to those who are trapped in those practices for generations. Ancestral worship is the same as visiting the graves, the place of the dead. It opens people to manipulations by strange, demonic spirits disguising as dead relatives. It is interesting that many cultures have their versions of connecting to the dead and hold their practices with high esteem. In some churches, people pray to dead saints or the apostles of the old thinking that their prayers can only be answered when they go through those saints. The deception of the enemy is intense and ingrained in many cultures, communities and societies.

In Ecclesiastes 9:5-6, it says, "For the living know that they will die, but the dead know nothing, and they have no reward, for the memory of them is forgotten. Their love and their hate and their envy have already perished, and forever they have no more share in all that is done under the sun."

The dead can never mediate for the living. Even the dead Samuel could not mediate for the living Saul before God. Only Jesus Christ is the mediator between God and the living. 1 Timothy 2:5 says, "For there is one God, and there is one mediator between God and men, the man Christ Jesus." This means the dead will never represent the living before God. Only Jesus Christ is the connection between the living and God. Those who do not have Jesus Christ have no representative and mediator in heaven.

In John 14:6, Jesus says, "I am the way, and the truth and the life. No one comes to the Father except through me."

I believe the church was committing the sin of necromancy by encouraging the congregants to visit the graves and engage with demonic spirits of the grave, thinking they are talking to their dead relatives, and they have the power to help the living, making it look like an acceptable spiritual practice to the ignorant and simple-minded. This is what made me think the dead are somehow alive and look after their living relatives as a connection between God and the families they came from. This was the work of Satan, who has deceived the world. Many cultures and traditions around the world embrace these kinds of deceptions. In John 16:11 (Amplified Version), Jesus Christ called Satan an evil genius who is already judged and condemned and his sentence is already passed. He is the father of lies and deception.

The Bible unequivocally says necromancy, meaning speaking to the dead, is a sin and an abomination to God. It is a form of idolatry and false worship. It is a painful thing to live a life without God. Remember, ignorance is not an excuse in the spirit realm. It can take a person to hell. The graveyard visits by the church were not of God. It was the work of Satan, the evil spirits and of witchcraft. Even people sleeping during the church service was the work of dark forces.

I think these kinds of extra-biblical customs and practices in the church makes necromancy and idolatry look acceptable. It makes speaking to the dead normal and look like a necessary spiritual practice. People end up wanting to worship the dead, sacrifice to them, hoping that they connect them to God and can help them in their day-to-day life. This was my impression until I came to know what the Bible says about the dead. In the church, many held this deceitful perspective. May the Lord God forgive us for such ignorance in the mighty name of Jesus Christ.

1 Timothy 4:1 says, "Now the Spirit expressly says that in later times some will depart from the faith by devoting themselves to deceitful spirits and teachings of demons."

In Hebrew 9:27, it says, "And just as it is appointed for man to die once, and after that comes judgment." Reincarnation is a lie of the devil.

There are many verses where God addresses this issue and the consequences of engaging with the dead. In Leviticus 19:31, it says, "Do not turn to medium or necromancers; do not seek them out, and so make yourselves unclean by them; I am the Lord your God." In Leviticus 20:6 God says, "And a person who turns to mediums and familiar spirits, to prostitute himself with them, I will set my face against that person and cut him off from his people." Even Jesus Christ when one of the disciples said to him that he must go and bury family before he can follow him, Jesus Christ said "Follow me, let the dead bury the dead" Matthew 8:21-22; Luke 9:59-60. The fruit of engaging mediums and the dead is curses in the lives of people for generations if they never repent and receive deliverance in the name of Jesus Christ and the power of the Holy Spirit.

After visiting the graveyard as a church, we would then go back to the church for a resurrection Sunday service. The actual church service after the procession always felt very spiritual and heavy to me, made my heart sore each time I recall how they killed Jesus Christ.

My first vision of Jesus Christ: I recall one Easter Sunday when we were back in the church for the service, the last time I attended the Easter service at that Anglican church, I was so heartbroken, sad, with tears in my eyes when I recall how they killed Jesus Christ. The Lord opened my eyes to see a vision. I saw Jesus Christ with the 12 Apostles seated around a big table. Their table replaced the altar of the church. Jesus Christ was seated on the side, and he looked at me and smiled. Then the vision closed. I asked my elder sister, who was next to me, if she had seen the same thing, and she said no. From that time, I could not speak about this experience to anyone. It was as if my tongue was locked and not permitted to speak about the vision. I did not understand the vision at that time. Now I believe that the Lord was saying to me, he is alive and not dead, that I should celebrate his resurrection and not mourn his death.

Over time, I forgot about the vision. It was not until I started seeking God and became interested in knowing what the Bible says and who Jesus Christ is that I remembered this vision and eventually was able to talk about it.

The memories of that day, from when we joined the procession until we were back in the church and the vision are still so vivid. Initially, when I became a born-again Christian, attending a Baptist church, I wanted to speak about the vision, but I thought that people would think that I was crazy or lying and would not believe me. No one spoke about any visions; they did not believe in any spiritual experiences, encounters or deliverance by the power of the Holy Spirit and often proclaimed with confidence that miracles had ceased and speaking in tongues was demonic. They did not know the power of the Holy Spirit or have any or deep understanding of the spiritual realm and how it affects our day to day lives. It was a cessation church, believing that the works of the Holy Spirit such as laying on of hands to pray for the sick and they shall be healed, deliverance in the name of Jesus Christ, speaking in tongues, casting out devils and demons, and many of the gifts of the Holy Spirit and of Jesus Christ, have ceased with the Apostles. One day I amassed enough courage and spoke to one of the daughters of the pastor about the vision and true, she looked at me like I was crazy. From that time on, I was ostracized and felt rejected especially by the pastor's family. I left the church and moved to another Baptist church.

Eventually I heard from the Holy Spirit in my heart that I needed deliverance and should come out of the Baptist church. I told the senior pastor of the church that I heard from the Holy Spirit that I needed deliverance. He said to me deliverance was of the devil and demonic. This was contrary to what Jesus Christ said in Mark 16:17-18 (NKJV) which states "And these signs will follow those who believe: In my name they will cast out demons, they will speak in new tongues, they will take up serpents; and if they drink anything deadly, it will by no means hurt them; they will lay hands on the sick and they will recover."

I chose to obey the voice of the Holy Spirit and came out of the Baptist church, and the rest is history. A whole new spiritual world opened. It became an experience that only Jesus Christ, by his power and the Holy Spirit, can take a person through and sustain them. It got intense beyond my wildest imagination. It was nothing I had ever known or heard. Even the two Baptist churches I had attended got exposed to me spiritually. I got to see the power of Jesus, the infallible word of God, the Bible, the power of the name of Jesus Christ, the power of the blood of Jesus Christ and the power of the Holy Spirit in action. The spirit realms became alive for me once I obeyed the instruction to come out of the Baptist church and seek deliverance. My relationship with God, Jesus Christ and the Holy Spirit moved to a new level. I felt the presence of the Lord more and heard more from him. Since then, I have seen Jesus again and even Satan and demons of all kinds.

I had to be delivered from wrong spiritual practices and beliefs. Before my deliverance, I received my share of torments from Satan, demons and witches after confessing Jesus Christ as my Lord and Savior. I needed to be spiritually strong and endure. I engaged in intense prayer and fasting. The Holy Spirit taught me the Bible and how to use it as a weapon of spiritual warfare. He also led me to some incredible ministers of the Gospel to learn from and for my deliverance. My deliverance was not a onetime event. It took time and visits to many countries. Eventually, I received my deliverance. God's word regarding judgement for iniquities, transgressions and sin is true. God is faithful to his word.

I came to understand Christianity in a new way and the power that lies in spirit-filled born-again Christian. I got to see for myself that deliverance, supernatural healing and speaking in tongues is of God and needed. I came to understand that Christianity is a practical relationship with God the Father, Jesus Christ and the Holy Spirit. It is not a religion. I now believe a true born-again Christian is a powerful, supernatural person, empowered by Jesus Christ through the Holy Spirit. I can confidently confirm that the work of the Holy Spirit has never ceased, and that Jesus Christ still baptizes those who believe with fire to carry out the great commission. He is truly the same yesterday, today and forever.

Church services in my early years: With regards to the church services, our Anglican church followed a structured pattern, mostly chanting from the catechism in a very slow-motion way, repeating or responding to the preacher. There was also singing from the hymn book. The hymns were mostly good. Although I cannot remember any of them, I liked hearing the congregation sing hymns. In my recollection, most services were boring, confusing as procedures were not really explained before the age of 16. I did not enjoy most services. I went to church because I thought it was the right thing to do, and it made me feel good to a point. Because I was a spiritually sensitive person, going to church made me feel spiritually connected.

I do not recall any Bible reading and teaching during the service. I believe that could be the reason we did not read the Bible at home. There was barely any prayer, only the book of common prayers or catechism chanting during the service. The congregation did not pray in the church. On most days, whenever I was in the church, I felt sleepy and embarrassed, and could not wait for the service to end. Most people slept throughout the service. I saw a lot more people, young and old, falling asleep and slumbering during the church services. Slumber and sleep during the church service can only be the work of dark forces, the work of demons. I have never seen a church where so many people were attacked by the spirit of sleep and slumber during the church service. I now know that sleeping during a church service is a spiritual attack on a person. It means the congregation in that Anglican church were spiritually attacked often.

I recall one Sunday, when I was in middle school, my younger sister, my cousin who grew up in our home and I were asked to go to church. We did not want to go. We were sluggish, so slow getting ready that by the time we left home, we were so late and ashamed. Our church services were normally 1.5 hours to 2 hours. On that day, we were about an hour late. One of my elder sister's friend lived in the same street as the church. We decided to rather go and visit them, have some tea then go back home and lie that we had been to church. When we got home, my mother asked what the announcements were, and we could not account. This is how our evil decision was exposed, and it was embarrassing. I do not remember what the consequences were, but we were strongly reprimanded.

My cousin was the instigator; she came up with the idea and we agreed. We cooperated and colluded in that wicked decision. I take full responsibility for this sinful act. I chose to cooperate with ungodly counsel. I have asked for forgiveness and know God has forgiven me. This kind of behavior is the product of religion and living in the flesh without any relationship with Jesus Christ and the influence of the Holy Spirit. It is the product of the lack of knowledge of God and the fear of God. Proverbs 9:10-12 says, "The fear of the LORD is the beginning of wisdom, and the knowledge of the Holy One is understanding." There was no wisdom at all in our decision.

My cousin really did not like church or anything to do with God. I have not seen or spoken to her in ages, and I believe she is still the same. Be careful the company you keep. I remember she once made a mockery joke about Jesus Christ and the woman at the well. Her comment disturbed me, and I never forgot it. Her joke shocked and hurt me, even though I was not born again yet and did not know or understand who Jesus Christ is. I was embarrassed by her comment and joke. I just knew it was wrong, disrespectful and unacceptable to God and that no one should joke like that about Jesus Christ. She insinuated that the story was false.

On my part, I just thought Jesus Christ was the ancestor of the Jews and not me, and that he did not know me. People also used to say he was the ancestor of the Jews, and I thought they were correct. Some used this twisted deception in our area to worship what they thought were their ancestors, their deceased relatives, while they were worshipping demons, familiar spirits posing as their relatives. This kind of worship was promoted, and many practiced it. I was clueless that Jesus Christ is the savior of the world and the deliverer of the lost.

The poor understanding of Christianity growing up shaped my worldview until I met the true Jesus Christ, and the Holy Spirit opened my eyes, understanding and ears. The experiences and events that unfolded in my life before I became a born-again Christian, a complete believer in Jesus Christ, the Word of God, the person of the Holy Spirit and the Bible are a testimony of the dangers of pseudo-Christianity.

Over time, as I became more aware of the spiritual realm as a born-again Christian, I began to witness to my family, exposing the realm of darkness we were exposed to unknowingly and therefore susceptible to spiritual attacks and manipulations. I lost most of my family members and friends in the world; some decided to distance themselves from me to this day. Choosing Jesus Christ truthfully and faithfully has come at a price for me. However, I will choose Jesus Christ again and again if I must choose daily. I have no regrets and I am more happier being in the Kingdom of God with the Lord than I ever was without Jesus Christ. In Matthew 16:24 (NKJV), Jesus Christ said to his disciples that "If anyone desire to come after me, let him deny himself, and take up his cross and follow me."

THE SPIRIT REALM: CHILDHOOD DECEPTIONS AND LIFE WITHOUT GOD

The enemies of God's love: Fear and Superstitions

Growing up, the spirit realm was beyond my comprehension. My understanding and awareness of the spirit realm, until I truly came to Christ by the power of the Holy Spirit, was limited, hazy and filled with fear. Fear is an enemy of faith and the opposite of Love. God is Love, and love casts away all fears. In 1 John 4:18 (NKJV), it says, "There is no fear in love; but perfect love cast out fear, because fear involves torment. But he who fears has not been made perfect in love." Fear is an enemy of God's love. Love comforts and encourages, while fear torments and discourages.

Because of fear, many people end up making the wrong decisions, going to the wrong places for help and making wrong covenants in the spirit, which in turn govern their lives in the physical. Fear makes even those who know God forget that God is love, loves them and that His love redeems.

Growing up, I heard a lot of mystical and mythical stories, fairytales and folklore, most of which revolved around Satan, evil spirits, witches and wizards and the fearful things they did to humans, especially at night. These stories used to fill me with fear.

There is one story I heard as a little girl that I remembered for a very long time because it was the scariest to me. I must say the storytellers, who were mostly our maternal grandmother and elderly people around us, were truly gifted in storytelling. Their actions and tone were captivating. The whole thing sounded true and alive. The story I recall vividly was about the giants who once roamed the earth, were cannibals and ate humans alive. They said those giants were also witches and would disguise themselves as a friend or relative when they knocked on someone's door. They would mimic their voices to fool the people inside the targeted house into opening the door. Once the person opened their door, they would capture them and eat them up. They made people disappear from the face of the earth. The graphic description of those giants made them sound like monsters, hateful, scary creatures who competed for existence on earth with human beings. They hated humans and regarded them as prey, dinner for their unquenchable thirst for human blood and meat. This story used to instill so much fear in me. They demonstrated this using the story of a little girl and her grandmother who lived in a village and practiced subsistence farming. The good part of the story was that the little girl eventually managed to fool the giants and got them killed to preserve her and her grandmother's lives.

Now I know the giants were demons. I think that the giants in the story were probably referring to the Nephilim spoken about in the Bible. Stories like this were worse than watching a scary movie. As I listened to those stories, I would play the whole scene like a movie in my mind. Each time I listened to those stories, I would feel very scared. My highly imaginative mind would run wild. I would imagine things. Those stories just planted fear and nothing else.

On top of hearing scary mythical stories, there were lots of scary mystical beliefs and superstitions. Supernatural, unexplained phenomena would also happen now and then. There were beliefs that witches and demons, even though we could not see them, were around to do evil to people all the time. This gave me the impression that the witches and evil spirits were pervasive, invisible creatures and monsters who were always in the environment, too powerful to overcome, and out to just destroy and kill people. The thought of them made me feel powerless, and I wanted to hold on to God for safety and protection. People used to advice that speaking the Lord's Prayer when evil comes to attack, is the solution. It is so funny how no one mentioned the protection they were receiving by visiting spiritual workers in darkness. The reason was that such practices were done in private, guarded closely as family secrets and never to be exposed to others. It was safer to speak openly about the Lord's Prayer because it was the truth and made people spiritually trustworthy.

There were also scary stories about the rain. We had a lot of rain each year, which made farming fruitful. Each time there was rainfall with thunderstorms, lightning was the biggest concern. Once the rain stopped, people would be curious to know if lightning killed anyone. It was believed that the rain could be manipulated by witchcraft to kill people with lightning, especially in the villages that had no electricity. Because of this, I came to dislike anything to do with villages because they were presented as dangerous zones where supernatural evil activities ruled, and reigned in people's lives. There was a notorious village, a few kilometers from our area. This village was known for its witchcraft prowess. This is where people died or were afflicted in mysterious ways that were beyond normal comprehension. In the area where we lived, I do not recall anyone being killed by lightning during thunderstorms. To avoid being a victim, we were told not to take a bath or take cover under a tree during rain with thunderstorms and lightning. In my little mind as a child, I could never imagine how rain, such a natural, God given blessing, could be used by evil people to cause harm. I didn't understand that spiritual component of rain. I recall also the stories about one queen in another village who could cause rain. She was called the rain queen, and her stories are still spoken about to this day. Now I know she had marine kingdom powers from darkness that helped her to make it rain whenever she wanted. Apparently, her subjects in the village where she ruled respected her highly and were scared of her supernatural powers. I bet some even worshipped her as their God.

There were some real fearful stories of what witches or mermaids could do when it rained. There was a river in the town where I grew up. It was believed that there was a mermaid in the river that was working with witches to cause the rain and death by lightning. That river was known to drown people and had a lot of crocodiles. I recall one neighbor's son who drowned in that river and was never found until this day, even after the river dried up. They said mermaids were taking those people to their other locations. So, I was afraid of that river and never wanted to get close to it, especially after the rain and when it was full.

I remember one time we had some seriously heavy rain with thunderstorms that lasted for hours and caused catastrophic damage and the worst floods ever. We were told that the storm was because the mermaid was changing locations, and had caused such torrential rain that no one could see it when it moved from one river to another. By the time the rain stopped, all homes, including our home, were flooded. I remember sitting on top of the dining table to avoid getting wet. Our living room was like a little dirty swimming pool. It was only later that they discovered that the poorly designed and installed drainage system in the town was responsible for the flooding from the rain. So, between the mermaids and poor municipal drainage, lives were lost and properties destroyed.

Superstition controlled beliefs, perspectives and controlled how people managed their lives. There were even suggestions that sometimes the rain was not real, that witches caused it to rain so they could kill someone with lightning. So, we never knew which rain was real and from God and which one was unreal and from the forces of darkness. It was like darkness covered the land, and witches and witchcraft had power over the elements of nature. Those stories glorified evil and not God. The fact that these are natural phenomena was discredited due to superstitious beliefs.

Superstition is an enemy of sound minds, judgment and truth and happened mostly because people were far removed from God, Jesus Christ and the Spirit of truth, the Holy Spirit. In the villages, it was worse than in the towns and cities. The argument was that electricity in the urban areas makes it impossible for witches to destroy us with lightning. Growing up, I really did not like the rain with thunderstorms because it created a great fear in my little mind and heart. I liked the quiet, soft, gentle rain because there were no dramatic stories associated with it. I still don't like thunderstorms and lightning.

The other thing was a whirlwind. They said that witches could cause a whirlwind and send it to a target house to steal, mainly food items and bring them to the witches' houses. We had frequent strong whirlwinds in our area since roads were unpaved at that time. In the villages, they said the problem was worse. There were creepy stories from villages. Hearing those stories, one would wonder if there were innocent people and households in the villages.

As I child, I lived in fear of evil spirits, rain, whirlwinds, witchcraft, darkness, dogs, cats, crawling creatures such as scorpions, crickets, cockroaches, and rats, which were a lot and behaved in a weird way. It was common to hear people say rats or other things ran in their ceilings at night, but they could not find them during the daytime. We were told that dogs and cats are used by witches as instruments of witchcraft, especially at night. I recall one morning, it was reported that a strange dog was found stuck at a certain house, unable to move until they made a noise and started stoning it. The dog ran away with people chasing it and tried to find refuge in people's yards, and our home was one of those yards. The dog was unusually big and skinny. They said the dog was sent to do witchcraft at the house where it was stuck.

Also, no one wanted any black cat around. They said witches could turn into animals, especially cats, to do their evil deeds. Generally, people in our township did not keep pets. All pets were suspects. It was peaceful and safer not to have any.

I recall between the ages of 4-7 being afraid of men who delivered coal in the neighborhoods. Most people in the township where I grew up used coal stoves, as they did not have electricity in their houses at that time or were managing their electricity bill. The men who delivered the coal were very dark skinned because of the coal they worked with throughout the day, and their dress coats were also marred with coal dust. The nature of their job made their appearances look quite unclean and their skin tones pitch black. Their sight frightened me. They gave me such a fright that each time I saw them, I would run uncontrollably into the nearest hiding place, such as the closet or under the bed.

I once came across them walking back home from elementary school. When we turned the corner, I saw the coal truck, and the men were offloading coal to deliver to some houses on that street. Although I had a lot of students walking with me, I did not feel safe. Fear captured me.

When we got closer to those men, I lost control. I ran into the nearest house through their kitchen to the bedroom and hid under the bed. Everyone was shocked. It was like something took control of me. That was not normal. It was spiritual.

As a child, I thought those men were not real human beings. They looked like scary monsters, ghosts to me. They reminded me of the evil monsters and demons I have heard of in the folklore stories my grandmother and older cousins used to tell us. Those men were just people and not evil monsters out to get me. I am sure they were just nice, civil citizens doing their work to feed their families and make a living.

Though I did not know fear was a spiritual issue, I recall my dad implying that it was and concerned about the level of fear I had.

Fear is a spirit. I had an intense, paralyzing fear in my childhood. I honestly do not know at what point fear came into me. From a tender age, I was afraid of many things for many years, and it was excessive at times until I became a born-again Christian and the Lord set me free.

The Bible says fear is of the devil and that "God has not given us a spirit of fear but of power, and of love and of a sound mind," 2 Timothy 1:7. There was no power, love or sound of mind in my reaction.

Though fear tormented me as a child, as I grew older, I developed and demonstrated a commendable level of courage and bravery in most areas of my life.

Because I suffered from fear, I learned a few lessons about the evil of fear and superstition. What I have learned about fear is that it can be restricted to some areas of a person's life and not permeate the entire parts of a person's life. It can be contained to specific areas or things.

Because it can be confined, people can live with fear for a very long time, if not forever, by avoiding things, people and places they are fearful of. A person could come across as courageous and brave in some areas, but have a paralyzing fear of something. If not dealt with spiritually in the name of Jesus Christ, it can multiply to affect a lot of areas in a person's life. The antidote to fear is faith. With faith, fear melts away. Faith is a gift God gives to human beings.

Every person has a measure of faith. However, a person's faith can be dormant where fear has taken over.

I have also learned that because fear is spirit, it can be transferred through birth or relations, such as the name one is given or the person naming the child. The strange thing is that my niece, whom I had named after me, and now dead, also had the same extreme fear of people of dark-skinned pigmentation. I also had a fear of domestic animals. My daughter, as young as 1 year of age, also exhibited a fear of domestic animals just as I did for a very long time. Fear is a spirit that transfers between people and in families.

I now know from experience that fear is a spirit, an evil spirit, a demon, that is transferable, especially where there is a soul tie, even just by being named after someone who has or had the spirit of fear. Fear can easily become a generational curse in the family. This also tells me that the things we take for granted, such as names, are not ordinary. They are spiritual and connect people spiritually, presenting spiritual inheritance in some cases. Be mindful of who or what you are named after. Fear is one of the ways that Satan and his demons used to access my life and the lives of many afflicted with the evil spirit of fear. Living in sin can be a breeding ground of fear.

The key question is, at what point did this spirit of fear enter my family? I do not believe that I, my daughter and niece were the only ones. I wonder what kinds of fear the grandmother I was named after had. My assumption is that when my predecessors turned away from God and worshipped other things, such as strange spirit beings through traditional practices or false religions, fear found its way into the family. Before I became spiritually awake, I used to think that it was because of the mythical stories the family elders used to tell us as kids that made me fearful. Now I believe that the main reason fear manifested was due to sin in my family foundation. Probably fear was just sitting there and moving around the family, waiting for an opportune moment to announce itself. Where there is sin, Satan and his evil agents find expression through and in the lives of sinners and their descendants. They do not care whether the person is a newborn baby or not. Remember, the word compassion is foreign to Satan and his evil spirits, demons. They possess whomever they will to express themselves and do their evil works. Where there is fear, there is darkness and malevolent beings that fuel and feed on it.

Living in fear is like living in a prison. As a young child, I could not walk alone or sleep alone in bed. I always felt that there was something or someone around, unsafe and fearful. I always wanted to be in the middle. The only time I could be alone was during the daytime, but another person had to be close by. This is funny because I was told that when I was a toddler, once I started crawling and walking, I liked being alone. They said I would go to the side of the house where it was quiet and had vegetation. They said I would normally disappear into the garden, and they would always find me eating peppers and tomatoes in the garden alone without any fear.

Even when I was a young teenager, I still liked being alone during the daytime and would not feel bored most of the time. However, whenever I felt bored, which was rare, I would cry. My niece, whom I had named after me, would also cry when she was bored.

With fear, you do not see the cage of your prison and the prison guards, but the hold on your spirit can feel so real, painful and overwhelming. Fear is an evil spirit, you cannot see it, but you know it is there, like another person in you, around you and having a hold on you. I have firsthand experience of the torments of fear.

Fear is a demon and needs to be cast out in the name of Jesus Christ by the Holy Spirit. It cannot be treated with medicine, psychiatry, psychology or positive affirmation because it is a spirit. Only affirming the word of God, which is also Spirit, can cast away the spirit of fear. Like any other evil, unclean spirit, fear needs to be dealt with using the name above it, and that name is Jesus Christ. I believe anyone who has experienced the torments of fear will appreciate God's consistent reminder to his children not to fear but be of good courage. Faith and courage go hand in hand. You need faith to move with courage, and you need courage to exercise your faith.

The Bible says God did not give us the spirit of fear, but of love, of power and of a sound mind; 2 Timothy 1:7. Again, the Bible says God did not give us the spirit of bondage to fear again, but the spirit by whom we cry ABBA Father; Romans 8:15.

In the Bible, many times God says, "Fear not, for I am with thee." Isaiah 41:10 (KJV) says, "Fear thou not; for I am with thee: be not dismayed; for I am thy God: I will strengthen thee; yes, I will uphold thee with the right hand of my righteousness." It takes faith to believe what God says, and it takes courage to trust God's word and promise. That is why the Bible says that without faith, no one can please God.

Fear breeds doubt. Where there is doubt, there is defeat and timidity. The love of God casts away all fear. Knowing that God is our Father who loves us, true and faithful to his promises, helps us not to fear, for we know that in any situation, God is there to help us overcome, to protect, to defend and to provide for us as he has promised.

Joshua was encouraged to take the children of Israel into the Promised Land by God amid cruel nations that wanted the complete destruction of the children of Israel. In Joshua 1:1-9 (NIV and NKJV), God told Joshua multiple times, "Be strong and courageous, because you will lead these people to inherit the land I swore to their ancestors to give them." "Be strong and of good courage; do not be afraid, nor be dismayed, for the Lord God is with you wherever you go. Be careful to obey all the law my servant Moses gave you; do not turn from it to the right or to the left, that you may be successful wherever you go."

I believe God repeated the words to Joshua because he knew it was easy for fear to creep in to interfere with God's purposes and promises to the children of Israel. Because Joshua believed God, the children of Israel reached and possessed the Promised Land without much opposition. God also told Joshua how to keep his strength and courage by obeying the law of God that Moses gave him. I believe God mentioned obedience to the law because he knew that in difficult situations, wrong wisdom can mislead innocent people.

This tells us that having the word of God in our hearts gives birth to faith and courage. It is impossible to have faith in God without the manifest word of God. Also, without the word of God in the heart, it is easy to look elsewhere for instructions in the face of opposition. I believe the absence of the word of God in the hearts of people in many parts of the world has given rise to alternative religions and practices people use for instructions on matters of life. When people are courageous and focused on what the word of God says, it becomes easy to press on even when the external conditions are unfavorable. Fear has no room, and therefore defeat and failure cannot be the outcome.

Fear is one of the weapons the enemy uses to connect people to himself and disconnect people from God, Jesus Christ and the Holy Spirit. Fear is an enemy of faith, and without faith no one can please God. Fear stops people from experiencing their full potential. It diminishes courage, boldness and confidence, which are the qualities humanity need to walk by faith.

Unfortunately, without the help of the Holy Spirit, a walk of faith can be epileptic. Again, without the Holy Spirit, any expression of faith can be arrogance, stemming from the flesh and very unreliable. Faith helps us to face our fears with humility and destroy pride and arrogance. Faith in God is a perfect antidote to fear, pride of the self and arrogance. The Bible says in Habakkuk 2:4 that "behold the proud, his soul is not upright in him, the just shall live by his faith." True faith humbles the person because the person knows that it is through the help of God that they had the faith to achieve success.

Imagine if David feared Goliath. David faced Goliath because he had complete faith in the Lord and His power to go to battle with him and give him victory. He announced in 1 Samuel 17:45 to Goliath that "I come against you in the name of the LORD of Hosts." The Lord destroyed Goliath, the giant, through the hands of David. Faith can help us move mountains, face giants, and achieve things unimaginable. God has given each of us a measure of faith, as written in Romans 12:3. To live on earth requires faith, as many things are unpredictable and we approach them by faith, knowingly or unknowingly.

Without God, fear can easily become a reality in a person's life. The presence of God in a person's life casts away all fear. I also did not know that fear is a sin before God because it is not of God. Fear does not come from God; it comes from Satan, the father of it and many other evil things that torment people. The only way to be made perfect in Love is by and through God, who is love. The Bible says those who fear are not made perfect in love and that love covers the multitude of sins. This includes the sin of fearfulness. In 1 John 4:18, it says, "There is no fear in love; but perfect love casts out fear, because fear involves torment. But he who fears has not been made perfect in love."

Due to his love for humanity, God sent his one and only begotten Son to come and redeem humanity and cover our multitude of human sins through the blood of Jesus Christ shed at Calvary, which washes away the sins of the world. Fear is included in the many sins that are washed away by the blood of Jesus Christ in the lives of those who believe and receive salvation through Christ Jesus.

Fear is a form of disobedience to God. Being fearful is not aligned with the image and the likeness of God in which humanity is created. Fear is such a serious matter to a degree that in the Book of Revelation 21:8 (KJV) it is written; "The fearful, and unbelieving, and murderers, and whoremongers, and sorcerers, and idolaters, and all liars, shall have their part in lake which burneth with fire and brimstone: which is the second death." Fear, just like disobedience to God, is a sin against God. The fearful are put in the same category as the unbelieving, murderers, sexually immoral, sorcerers, witches and liars, which are all acts of disobedience to God. Living in fear is limiting and can easily turn people away from God, cause them to do evil, such as seeking the help of sorcerers and witches when trouble comes or persists and can also cause people to kill and lie.

Although, as a child, I also heard about the Holy Spirit, the narratives about the evil spirits were much louder. I grew up in a place that was quite religious and known even to this day for its witchcraft practices. The town and villages around carried an unpleasant, dark presence and needed salvation. There were conventional churches and African apostolic churches, which were very traditional in their practices. I recall one house church near our home where they had a night vigil every Saturday night with loud drums. They played their drums all night until the morning and wore mostly blue and white uniforms. Whatever they did throughout the night was a secret. I think the loud drums were to conjure spirits. There were many places like that. I wonder why they called themselves Christians because they were not. They were rather a concoction of traditional practices with a Biblical flavor. I always wondered to this day how I and some others survived that place and are where we are today.

Their practices of loud drums and dancing claiming spiritual connection were no different from what I had seen before performed by workers of darkness. I had seen such drums and dances during the daytime performed by witchdoctors, and people who did ancestral worship and those coming back from a month long (June) initiation on the mountain for circumcision, saying they are possessed by spirits. They would do such things publicly for passersby to watch, and they were a bit scary…

The town and villages needed salvation so much that one Saturday morning, the town woke up to find the inscription "JESUS" written in big, bold white paint on top of a big rock on the mountain. The inscriptions could be seen from every side of the town. I did not know what to think or what it meant. People were shocked. Looking back, I believe it meant that JESUS CHRIST cared deeply about our place and the people of that land. It was a reminder that the land needed the saving grace of our Lord Jesus Christ. In due season, Jesus Christ brought salvation, healing, deliverance and redemption in my life and the lives of many.

FAULTY SPIRITUAL FOUNDATIONS

"By Their Fruit, You Shall Know Them"

Faulty spiritual foundations are real and pervasive. The foundation upon which a house is built determines its strength and durability. In the case of humans, people are houses, and their family lineages are the foundations upon which they stand. The Bible in Psalm 127:1 (KJV) says, "Except the LORD build the house, they labor in vain that build it; except the LORD keep the city, the watchman waketh but in vain." This is very true of all humans. If the house or a person is not built upon Jesus Christ and watched over by him, the house or the person will eventually fall, even if they do things to keep it standing.

Growing up, I heard stories about witchcraft, but never realized that it was under my nose, considering the practices of many families in the society, which were not built upon Jesus Christ and were rebellious to God's commandments and word. I guess many engaged in those practices, unaware of the deep spiritual meaning and consequences that would affect generations in their lineages. I have observed that many families suffered some repercussions such as lack of marriage in the lives of their children, teenage pregnancies, single parenthood, cruel sudden deaths, pre-mature deaths, drunkenness, abusive partners, evil attacks in dreams and in waking state, fear, hatred, disunity, children outside wedlock, stagnation, incurable illnesses, limitation, rejection, anti- Christ spirit in the families, madness and many other unpleasant experiences and curses.

In society, there were a lot of strange occurrences. There were mad and mentally disturbed people, abnormal people, deformed people, cruel criminals, women beaters, killings through knife stabbing for night riders who lived a life of wild parties, clubbing and drunkenness, strange voices and movements outside in the night and many other strange things.

I recall the time when a strange dog moved from house to house in the morning, and people chased it down with stones, saying it was a witchcraft dog that failed to return to its home after doing evil in the night. The other time, there was a woman in the morning who people wanted to stone to death because they said she was caught naked outside someone's home, where she had gone to do witchcraft. People also liked declaring death on their adversaries with the saying, "Hold the sun that it does not go down, because if it goes down, you are going down with it." After such a declaration, typically their adversaries will suddenly die from strange causes. Many families were suspected of practicing witchcraft, and people lived in fear of being bewitched. Life was like walking on eggshells, too careful not to break them. There was no freedom on the inside, even though people carried on like nothing was happening.

I believe that due to the absence of the Holy Spirit, the Spirit of the living God, the spirits that filled the land were evil and held people captive. The Bible says in 2 Corinthians 3:17 (NKJV) that "Now the Lord is that Spirit, and where the Spirit of the Lord is, there is liberty."

For a long time, though I feared witchcraft, I did not understand what it entailed. I thought most people were just traditional in their outlook, embracing their traditions, which were important for their survival. To me, traditional practices did not qualify to be called witchcraft or spiritual. It was just life that others chose. I got to a point where I sort of believed witchcraft did not exist because I had never seen a witch. I did not realize that practitioners of traditions were spiritual and in cohorts with evil spirits. People around me generally believed that witchcraft was real and had stories to support that.

Some people practiced their traditional beliefs openly, and some hid them. I now know those practices were of the devil and witchcraft in nature. There were even a few houses in the area that people said were not to be trusted, and the walkway near those houses was to be avoided as they were believed to practice evil. They said that they picked up people's footprints and used them to bewitch them. Kids from those families were also isolated, resented and despised in school. People did not talk to them. Those kids, in turn, separated themselves and socialized with a few friends who were also suspected of evil practices.

One of our next-door neighbors also had lots of strange traditional practices, which were mostly performed very early in the morning or in the evening once the sun went down. Their ritual practices looked and felt very dark in nature. They, too, were known to be witches, though we spoke to them. I think I only stepped inside their home once or twice and was shocked at how cold and dark it felt. The fact that they were poor did not help. There is a saying that were there is witchcraft, poverty can be the order of the day, that witchcraft brings poverty in people's lives. My family provided for them quite a bit. My parents were very giving. There were a lot of families which seemed to be more on the dark side in our neighborhood, especially those who did not go to any church. They called us the church people.

There was a clear, visible social and economic distinction between families which attended church and those who did not. Those who attended church were mostly professionals, a bit well-off, socially acceptable and discreet in their traditional beliefs and practices than those who did not go to church. It does not mean the churched people were not doing the same things as the unchurched. They were just secretive and discreet. The churched and unchurched were mostly two sides of the same coin.

Religion or church attendance did not make people stop their cultural, traditional practices, which are all abominations to God, sinful and demonic for the most part. I think that people were religious, attended churches, but held on to their traditional practices because conventional churches did not give practical solutions to their spiritual dilemmas and challenges. To resolve spiritual issues, people looked to the devil by visiting witchdoctors, doing ancestral worship, visiting graveyards of their deceased relatives and many other things. I believe they just did what their ancestors did before the advent of Christianity in the land. The fruit of those who attended church was no different from that of those who did not. Matthew 7:16-20 (KJV) says, "Ye shall know them by their fruits. Do men gather grapes of thorns or figs of thistles?. Even so, every good tree bringeth forth good fruit, but a corrupt tree bringeth forth evil fruit. A good tree cannot bring forth evil fruit, nor can a corrupt tree bring forth good fruit. Every tree that bringeth not forth good fruit is hewn down and cast into fire." These Bible verses speak to the depth of life.

I take the tree in the parable to mean a family, and the fruit to be the descendants and offspring. The root of the tree is the person's lineage. It takes a while for a tree to produce fruit. When the tree is planted, you never know if it is good or corrupt until it produces fruit. Just like in a family, when sins enter, the family may not see the impact and consequences of the sins in the generation that committed them. That generation may see good fruit from the labor of their sins. The root may take a while before it starts producing evil fruit. This means it can take a while to see the consequences of sins in the family. If the root of the family is defiled, the foundation is faulty, and the family will eventually suffer and crumble. Psalms 11:3 (NKJV) says, "If the foundations are destroyed, what can the righteous do?

The sins in the families destroy the foundations and the roots of their lineages. Those unrepented sins over generations create faulty foundations. This explains why there are generational curses, and even if someone is born again, they may need deliverance from family foundational issues and generational curses. Even though the family goes to church, portraying a Christian appearance with well-behaved, academically gifted children, they may find themselves embracing dark practices when trouble comes in the name of tradition and culture because church attendance or being born again does not destroy generational curses and repair the faulty foundations. The family demons and established evil covenants in the family keep on fighting the spiritual freedom of those who choose to be Christians. A Christian still needs spiritual deliverance to breaks curses and the yokes of faulty family foundations in order to see the blessings that come with putting one's trust in the Lord. If they don't, the children may notice in their adult years that the fruits they have reaped are somewhat like the ones of those who never went to church or call themselves Christians. If these children who have become Christians choose to never get delivered, the curses in their foundation brought about by sins will persist and intensify from generation to generation until people begin to receive deliverance and be separated from family curses. Be not deceived, God is not mocked; for whatsoever a man soweth, that shall he also reap as it is written in Galatians 6:7 (KJV). The good thing is that receiving and putting one's trust in Jesus Christ qualifies a person to break generational curses and establish a new family foundation ruled by the Holy Spirit. The evil tree would need to be uprooted completely, and a new tree with new roots planted to change the trajectory of the fruit. To change people's lives, new seeds would need to be planted in their lives. The evil foundation would have to be demolished completely, and a new foundation poured in. The Bible says Jesus Christ is the vine, and those who believe in him are the branches. Trusting and believing in Jesus Christ and doing his will produce good fruit. Jesus Christ's will is that demons should be cast out of people, divine healing be administered and the power of His name and the Holy Spirit manifested in the lives of born-again Christians. He said born again Christians should let their light shine before men that when they may see their good works, they would glorify the Father in heaven (Matthew 5:16). True deliverance and healing in the name of Jesus Christ and the power of the Holy Spirit glorifies our Father in heaven.

Although people would speak about the evil darkness and witchcraft in the community, speaking about demons seemed off-limits. It was not a common point of discussion, even in the church we attended, because people were afraid of them. People preferred to pretend like demons were not real and did not exist. Looking back, I realize that there were a few clear demonic activities and some demon-possessed people in the society where I grew up. Reading the Bible about the work of Jesus Christ, where he was casting out demons, his teachings and healings of the multitude, opened my eyes to realize that I had grown up seeing demon-possessed people. However, at that time in society, there was no known servant of God or a church equipped to cast the demons out of those who were possessed and bring them to salvation. Most people sought help from witchdoctors or false prophets and churches, the agents of Satan. They went to them as their first point of call. However, cases of demon possession got worse and increased. As written in the Bible, Satan cannot cast out Satan.

This was well articulated by Jesus Christ in Matthew 12:24-26 when his enemies, the Pharisees, accused him of casting out the devils by the spirit of Beelzebub, saying "This fellow does not cast out demons except by Beelzebub, the ruler of the demons." Jesus, knowing their thoughts he said to them, "Every kingdom divided against itself is brought to desolation, and every city or house divided against itself shall not stand. And if Satan cast out Satan, he is divided against himself, how shall then his kingdom stand?." It therefore goes without saying that a worker of the dark art can never set anyone free from demons. They are of the same cloth and work together to keep their kingdom going. As a result, those who were possessed by evil spirits in society traumatized the neighborhoods. They terrorized whoever was unfortunate enough to come across their path. The false churches and witchdoctors could not help them because they belonged to the same kingdom as demons.

Many people and families were in bondage. It was like there was a dark current moving about daily, a dark blanket giving a dark presence that people could not quite discern or see with their naked eyes but was very alive. Inside our home, we would find scorpions in the pantry, lots of cockroaches and bedbugs in some bedrooms, moving things on the roof at night, and lizards in some bedrooms. We once had a visitor who had bedbugs. The war against bedbugs was successfully won eventually, but the war against cockroaches yielded temporary wins. To this day, bedbugs and cockroaches are my worst pet peeves. I detest them.

Faulty family foundations and lineages of evil doers predispose people to evil attacks, evil spirits, witchcraft, Satan, demons, monitoring spirits, spiritual spouses, addictions, wayward living, mental health issues, incurable illnesses, child development issues, and many other unpleasant experiences. The faulty family foundations can come because of the predecessors, parents, or individuals themselves having been involved with witchcraft, visiting such workers of darkness as occultic priests, witchdoctors and psychics, practicing new age, yoga and necromancy, attending occultic religious churches and practices, the list is endless.

I, too, had my share of the results of faulty foundations. When I was in higher elementary school, on one fateful day, 2 of my friends and I decided to go to one of my friends' aunts, who lived closer to our school, at the foot of the mountain that had the inscription "JESUS" on it. It was during a 15-minute short break. We went there to eat and pay by washing dishes. By the time we finished eating and washed the dishes, the 15-minute school short break was over. We were scared to return to school late and be punished. I don't know what we were thinking. It was a given that a 15-minute break could not accommodate walking to a place outside school. So, probably a 10–15-minute walk, eat, wash dishes and take another 10-15 minutes to walk back.

Realizing that we were late, we decided to rather play a tennis game and go back during the 30-minute break. As we were playing, at one point, I couldn't catch the ball. It slipped through my hands in the direction of the mountain. I ran to go get the ball. I was barefoot. When I picked up the ball, I saw something that looked like a snakeskin. I had never seen a snake with my naked eye before. I said to my friends, "Hey, this looks like a snakeskin." They came running to see what I was talking about. When I moved my feet, I realized that I had stepped with my right foot on the head of the snake. It did not bite me. We screamed, and some men came to kill and burn it. I never told my family. A few years later, I developed an unusual rough-looking skin on my chest that looked like snakeskin. It started small and kept on growing for years. I recall someone telling me that it means that the snake I had stepped on when I was young had breathed on me to release poison instead of biting me. My family thought the rough, lizard/snake-like looking skin was due to eating canned fish, which was one of my favorite foods. My chest looked very bad. I used to hide it with clothes.

At one point in my first year in the university, after taking a shower in the communal bathroom, wrapped in a towel, I stood at the faucet to look at the mirror. My chest was not covered. One lady walked in and was shocked to see the skin on my chest. She then told me that Selsun Blue would heal me. She told me her mother was a nurse and used Selsun Blue to help people with the same condition, and told me what it was. It is a dandruff shampoo with a very strong smell. I believed her because I was desperate for healing. I decided to try her solution. I bought it and used it. It had a cold, burning sensation to it. Eventually, that skin disappeared and never resurfaced. I believe it was God's intervention to heal me in his own way. God's ways are not our ways. Even when we are sinners, he shows us mercy and compassion.

The other thing I suffered due to faulty foundation was a sudden feeling of fatigue on the crown of my head out of the blue. This happened frequently, especially when I was in social engagements. I would feel very tired of speaking and really fatigued in my jaw and crown. The crown of my head would beat up and down so strongly, like the heart pumping fiercely. When this happened, I would not want to talk or be around anyone. It always came so suddenly and made me come across as unfriendly and changeable like unpredictable weather. I would normally withdraw from social interaction and just wanted to be quiet. The fatigue I felt was extraordinary. Again, I never told anyone in my family. As I got older, it got less frequent than when I was a teenager. This was an evil attack. I believe I experienced that because when I was an infant, my parents did what they called strengthening of the crown on my head.

This kind of strengthening was done to all my siblings when they were infants. It was a common practice in the community. They would use the services of a witch doctor or a priest from a church that mixed the Bible with tradition to perform the ritual. They would use a razor blade to create an opening on an infant's crown and then put some concoction of herbal medicines, and then cover it with some red or black rubbing stuff. I believe this was what caused the condition I experienced in my teenage years. When I came to know Jesus Christ, started reading the Bible and prayed, mainly spiritual warfare prayers, the evil attack on the crown of my head stopped completely. I thank Jesus Christ for delivering me from this. Such strengthening is an intense spiritual ritual that I believe initiates infants to the kingdom of darkness. it is like handing your child over to darkness in the name of tradition and following in the paths of the ancestors. I wonder if parents understood the spiritual meaning and consequences of such practice on the lives of their children later in life.

Another experience due to faulty foundation happened in the 2nd year in university. I recall one day I decided to take a nap during the daytime. This was out of character. I do not recall whether my roommate was there or not. I had a strange dream that remained vivid to me to this day. Today, with what I have come to know about the spiritual realm, the dream was quite serious and very spiritual. I dreamed my deceased maternal grandfather and grandmother, whom I am named after, came to me to tell me that I will have more luck in life. They spoke in my ethnic language. What they said could be translated as saying blessings or fortune. They said, "My child, you will have lots and lots of blessings." They faded away, repeating lots and lots and lots, and I woke up from the dream. The dream was confusing and felt real. This dream remained in my memory, and I always wondered about it. I never told my family about it.

It was my first experience dreaming about a deceased relative. A part of me wanted to believe the dream, and another part was doubtful and confused. I could never forget this dream. Because of my spiritual background, I thought it was normal to dream of deceased relatives and get a word from them. I did not know God forbade such contacts. I did not know that the dead cannot have contact with the living. It is the truth I found in the word of God that helped me to discard the dream because I came to know it was false, it was evil spirits and a lie of the devil to deceive me, so he could trap me in darkness. Those were familiar spirits masquerading as my grandparents. The faulty family foundation had opened me up to receiving such deceptive dreams from the enemy.

The Bible says the dead are not aware of what is going on in the earth. They do not have a memory of those they have left behind. Ecclesiastes 9:5-6 (NKJV) says that "For the living know that they will die; but the dead know nothing, and they have no more reward. For the memory of them is forgotten. Also, their love, their hatred, and their envy have now perished; nevermore will they have a share in anything done under the sun."

This means that the dead do not know anything about the living. Death is a permanent separation between the dead and the living. As the Bible says, the dead have no further reward, and even the memory of them disappears. They lose their memory of things and people they have left behind. They do not remember anything about what and who they have left behind. What and who they loved, as well as what and who they hated and envied, perish with them, and they no longer have a part in anything that happens on earth.

Jesus Christ also gave a parable of Lazarus and the rich man in Luke 16:24-26. The rich man who died and was tormented in hell, in a place of eternal torment, wanted his brothers on earth who were living in sin to be warned about the realities of sin and hell. In the parable, the rich man asked Father Abraham to send Lazarus to his father's house to warn his brothers about hell. He was told the dead cannot come back to warn or talk to anyone about their life on earth.

So, any appearance of the dead in the dream is just the devil wanting to plant tares in people's lives, forge evil covenants and mislead them. The devil can do this because somewhere somehow, there is an evil altar that is speaking in the life of the person. The altar could have been established by the person themselves, their family or ancestors. In

Matthew 13:25, Jesus Christ told us in a parable that "but while men slept, his enemy came and sowed tares among the wheat and went his way. But when the grain had sprouted and produced a crop, then the tares also appeared." This tells us that the evil plans of the devil can be planted in a person's life in a dream while sleeping. The enemy plants spiritually because the dream world is a spiritual world. The enemy could be witches and people of darkness, demons, Satan and all evil spirits. The evil the enemy plants can take a long time before it shows in a person's life. It goes without saying that dreams are not ordinary.

Dreams are spiritual and deal with the spiritual world and spiritual beings. Dreams can even be prophetic. It is unwise to dismiss dreams. A person can know their spiritual makeup through their dreams. Many people in the Bible overcame because of the messages that came through dreams. Before I was born again, I was able to see things in dreams that came to pass. Once I was born again and filled with the Holy Spirit, I was able to see witches, demons, Satan and many other things in the dream and dealt with them. I was also able to see Jesus Christ and receive godly guidance in the dreams. With Christ, the Holy Spirit is my reliable, dependable and present help, I am able to receive instructions even when I am awake.

In Matthew 1:20-25, 2:12-13, 21, during the conception of Jesus Christ, his birth and toddler years, dreams played a big role in directing Joseph and Mary. Joseph was told in a dream to marry Mary, flee to Egypt from Herod, who wanted to kill baby Jesus, return from Egypt and move to Galilee. Even the Magi were warned through a dream not to go back to Herod but to use another route back to their country. These dreams were profound with extraordinary results. Because of these dreams, Herod never killed Jesus, and today many are saved because Joseph and the Magi accepted and obeyed the messages in the dreams. The good thing is that the messages they had received in their dreams were from God and not the devil. Joseph was warned of the devil's plans ahead of time and was able to circumvent them all. God is powerful and knows everyone's plans, including those of the devil. God gives us dreams to warn us of impending dangers, and people and the devil also gives people dreams. Dreams from God turn out to be true, align with the word of God and are without sorrow. People need to accept dreams from God and act on them. Dreams from God are a gift and a blessing from God. As the Bible says in Proverbs 10:22 (NKJV), "The blessing of the LORD makes one rich, and He adds no sorrow with it." As stated above, Satan also gives dreams.

However, dreams from the devil, though they may have inspiring messages, are deceptions and come with sorrow. A person can dream of eating great food at a party with their loved ones. The loved ones who appear in dreams could be familiar spirits feeding the person sorrow, such as sickness and failure in life. Most people who are witchdoctors normally testify that the message to become a witchdoctor came through dreams in an appearance of their deceased relatives, typically their grand or great grandparents, their ancestors. As stated earlier, entities like a person's ancestors in dreams are evil spirits called familiar spirits. These are spirits familiar with a person's lineage and can fool the current generation into trapping them in an evil path. Evil experiences and afflictions, such as sicknesses, can be planted in people's lives in dreams while they are sleeping. The evil plantation can take place when someone is young, and the sickness or evil experiences manifest in their adulthood. Spiritual programming can be done in dreams. The dreams from the devil always contradict the word of God and need to be rejected in the name of Jesus Christ and cancelled by the blood of Jesus Christ. When a person does something, accepts, rejects or overcomes things in the dream, that becomes the covenant either with God or with the enemy. Covenants established in dreams hold legal rights in the spirit realm and can cause those things to manifest in the physical realm. The Holy Spirit is a great help during the dream state to overcome evil attacks. When a person gets up, they need to either agree or reject whatever they saw or did in the dream to stop it from manifesting or allow it to manifest. Dreams are dynamic, as one can have a dream about or relating to other people. They still need to pray for or against the dreams on behalf of those people. However, only born-again Christians can really deal with the dreams effectively, as one needs the name of Jesus Christ, the blood of Jesus Christ and the Holy Spirit to destroy evil works or accept the good things they saw in their dreams. The covenant blood of Jesus Christ destroys any other covenants the person might have entered into during their dream state. Born-again Christians can call on the name of Jesus Christ and apply the blood of Jesus Christ against the evil dreams and the schemes of the devil in their lives.

Jesus also told us that the solution to dealing with tares the enemy plants in people's lives during the dream state is to get them burned by the fire of God.

When I dreamed about my maternal grandparents, I did not know those were familiar spirits with their lies and deception. I also did not know that immediately when I woke up, I needed to reject and cancel that dream in the name of Jesus Christ and plead the blood of Jesus Christ against it and ask God to burn those beings who appeared as my grandparents, their tares and whatever evil they had planted in my life with his fire. How could I have known what to do if I was not a born-again child of God who knows the word of God and has the help of the Holy Spirit?

As stated earlier, the dead have no ability to help the living. The enemy, Satan, can fool people through dreams to get them to agree and enter into covenants they should not enter. 2 Corinthians 11:14 (NLT) says, "Even Satan disguises himself as an angel of light." In Isaiah 8:18-20 (NLT), it says, "Someone may say to you, 'Let's ask the mediums and those who consult the spirits of the dead. With their whisperings and mutterings, they will tell us what to do'. But should not people ask God for guidance? Should the living seek guidance from the dead?"

In Deuteronomy 18:10-13 (KJV) and (NKJV) it says, "There shall not be found among you anyone who makes his son or daughter to pass through the fire, or one who uses or practice divination or witchcraft, or an observer of times or an enchanter, or a witch, or a charmer, or a consulter with familiar spirits, or a wizard, or a necromancer. For all that do these things are an abomination unto the Lord. Thou shalt be perfect with the Lord thy God." It is very clear that no one should talk to a deceased person when awake or in a dream while sleeping. This is an insult to the Lord and the epitome of darkness.

Dreaming about my deceased maternal grandparents was a demonic activity. It was an evil attack on my life, intended to defile me and my destiny in Christ. But to those who are perishing and love darkness, this kind of dream will be received with joy. It will be a welcome dream. God forbids this contact. Now I know, those were not my grandparents but demons. They were familiar/family spirits that were following me around. Familiar spirits are evil spirits that came into the family at some point because of sin and stay with the family for generations as sin persists, and there is no Jesus Christ in the family. They know the family well, the individual members' characters and can influence many of the lives of the family members or lineage. They tend to monitor family members from generation to generation and express their evil desires, such as lying to people that they are called into such things as witchdoctors, false prophets and take people to false churches. They can even influence the choices a person makes to align those choices with their evil desires for generations, even if those evil desires are not obvious and the choice looks like a blessing. They can even attract friends and partners into a person's life who are not really the best, even if those friends and partners look like the best matches. These spirits are responsible for fornication in people's lives because fornication defiles the body and opens a person up to more evil spirits in their lives. The human connections, such as friendships that are instigated by those evil spirits, will typically fade away over time when the person comes to Christ, unless those connections come to Christ too, then they can be sustainable.

GOD'S GRACE AND MERCY

God's grace and mercy to humanity are so great, and no amount of the enemy's tricks can hinder his mercy and grace in a person's life. Romans 9:18 (NIV) says, "Therefore God has mercy on whom he wants to have mercy." God gives grace and mercy to humanity even when they reject him or are lost in darkness. I had experienced such grace. God showed me grace since I was a child. I believe those familiar spirits that masqueraded as my maternal grandparents were aware of the unusual, supernatural help the Lord had been giving me since I was a child. I guess they wanted to take advantage of my ignorance and lack of knowledge. They wanted to lie just so I could trust them. I was not aware of the existence of familiar spirits at that stage in my life. I got that dream a year after my university fees were miraculously paid.

Some of the grace of God I experienced was when I was a child with mumps that refused to recede. They became stale. They distorted my face and my jawline. People used to mock me because of how I looked. My jawline looked like it had tennis balls. It was a little painful and hurtful when other kids mocked me, especially because when I was a baby, I had won a baby beauty contest a few times. I had a cheerful, beautiful baby face. Now, a few years later, my face was distorted and looked different from what it used to look as a baby because of the mumps. I craved healing but did not know how I was going to receive it and from whom. My parents didn't know what else to do.

Typically, when a child got mumps, they would put a tight cloth around their face to protect the mumps from being exposed to air. It was believed that exposure would cause them not to heal. A calabash would then be placed in a tightly closed room where a child would untie the cloth and put their face in the calabash and chant an incantation saying "mumps, mumps, go back into the pot." It was believed that this healing process was the solution and should take about a week. In my case, it failed. It did not work. After 2 weeks or so, doing this process, my parents decided to remove the cloth and let it be. My face was left with tennis ball-looking bumps on both sides next to my ears. It was an unpleasant look that attracted unwanted attention everywhere I went. I had to be strong. However, I rejected defeat and cried inside for healing.

The Lord came through for me. About a year or 2 later, during the school holidays, I was paging through a magazine. I was not reading because I did not know how to read yet. I saw an ointment, and something in me said this would heal the receded mumps. I showed my mother the ointment in the magazine, told her I believed the ointment would heal me. I asked her to buy it for me, and she agreed. I applied it to those receded mumps, and they disappeared in no time. I was overjoyed. That was a miracle to me. My face was restored. I believe God showed me mercy and brought this healing.

Another help and miracle I believe came from the Lord was a mysterious way my 1st year university fees were paid.

The mercy of God means exactly that. We don't have to buy it or do anything to earn it. It is his mercy and grace that have taken me from place to place, from strength to strength, from hopelessness to hopefulness, from misery to joy, even when I did not qualify as a sinner. "He makes His sun to rise on the evil and the good and sends His rain on the just and the unjust," Matthew 5:45. The just are the righteous, and the unjust are the unrighteous. I believe the evil are those who live their lives in the world as if God does not exist, worship the wrong god or gods and are without Christ and even reject the gospel. The good are the born-again Christians who do the will of God and keep his commandments and ways. Jesus Christ, who is God and has created all humans, is very merciful to all. He has shown me mercy even when I lived my life without him as an unjust and unrighteous person.

During my first year in university, my academic performance was very poor. I had no hope of passing most of my modules. I was also owing a lot of tuition and accommodation fees, almost all of my fees. I had a big student debt. I did not have any sponsorship, scholarship or bursary. In the last term of that year, about 3 months before the university closed, I decided to travel over 2000km on a 3rd class train coach to the big city, the economic hub of the country, to knock door to door at companies and ask them to pay my university fees. I had nothing to show them because my results were not impressive. I went by faith. No company promised to help. They had nothing to support their decision to invest in me. Even though no promises were made, I left my student number and the name of my university. It was a brave, courageous and intimidating move. I didn't overthink it, which helped.

About 2 days before the university closed, I decided to go to the student administration office and get my fee statement. I got a really nice surprise. The university administration manager called me into her office to let me know that someone from another company, who called about a week ago had paid all my outstanding balance. It was a huge balance. Apparently, the person who called the university mentioned that I had come a few months before and asked them to pay my tuition and accommodation fees. The person asked the university not to tell me the name of the company because they did not want me to come back. I was exhilarated. I could not fathom what I had just heard. To this day, I do not know who paid my first-year university fees. I got my results printed out on that day. This was just the mercy and the grace of God. It was a miracle.

When I left the administration office, a bee blew my bubble. I got bitten by a bee on my left eye. It was very painful. I was walking with a friend who knew what to do. She removed the bee stinger, and the pain subsided.

I was ashamed to show my results to my parents. My parents were disappointed in me. They thought I should move to another university, but then they changed their minds. I was embarrassed and disappointed for disappointing my parents. During this time, when I was home, my friend from school was visiting a German homoeopath regularly for her heart condition. I spent my university holidays accompanying her to the homoeopath, who also told me my heart valves were weak. I didn't receive any treatment from him.

During this time, one day, when I was preparing food for the family, my thumb got cut by a kitchen knife. It was a very small cut. Initially, it was like nothing happened. There was no pain. A few days later, the cut got worse, started bruising with pus and changed color. My thumb was looking rotten, and the pain was intense at night. I could not sleep due to the pain. I would cry all night long. Whenever I went to the clinic, they told me there were two options: to cut off my thumb or let it burst out on its own. I chose the latter and endured extreme pain. The cut was so small for my thumb to respond the way it did. The knife must have had poison. Our neighbor told me it was witchcraft and that my thumb was afflicted with a demonic wound. I didn't know what she was talking about and ignored her. By the mercy of God, one day when I was sleeping, the wound burst, and all the pus flew out. The pus was repulsive, had many colors. I was so excited and could not wait to go to the clinic in the morning. The pain disappeared immediately when the wound burst. It was amazing and joyful. I was healed without any medication or any remedy. The scar from that wound is still visible after many years.

At the end of the holiday season, my parents showed me mercy and allowed me to go back to the university. I came back with a great determination to pass and pass well. I fulfilled my promise. I passed very well and never lacked money to pay for my undergraduate and post-graduate degrees. Support came in supernatural ways.

From my second year of university onwards, I did very well. My performance allowed me to secure a job at the university. From that time onward, I always had a job on campus and during the holidays at a public library. I was also approved for a university loan from a company set up by the government to help less privileged students. Life was good. After graduating with my first degree, the public library offered me full-time employment, but I turned it down. I did not want to work in a library or museum. By God's grace and mercy, I managed to secure a full-time job within a few months after graduating with a reputable company. I was offered a job by two reputable companies at the same time. Deciding was not easy, and I am grateful I chose the company I went to.

I bought my first house, a car, got a promotion into management, as well as registered for a master's degree in business administration from the first company I worked for within the first two years of my employment after university. All these happened in a miraculous way. The company just had a lot of great benefits for its employees. They paid for my driving lessons, hired a driving teacher for me and loaned me a car to attend my MBA classes at the business school at night because I did not have my own car. They paid for my very expensive

MBA program. They also offered to pay off the student loan balance I had when I graduated in exchange for working for them for five years. I refused because I thought their offer would tie me down for five years. That was short-sightedness on my part. It was a great offer. I ended up paying the balance with interest from my pocket. I regretted refusing the offer.

My first employer had a housing financing program that allowed employees to take out a mortgage at very low interest rates. I decided to take advantage of the program. When I bought the house, I did not understand the company's process of buying a house. I just followed my intuition and faith. I applied and expected to be approved. I didn't know there was a wait list, and the process could take a few years before receiving approval to buy. After a few months of not hearing from the housing business unit, I decided to pay them a visit, go in person to follow up. On that fateful day, I bumped into a distant friend I had met when I was in university. He was the Managing Director responsible for the housing division. He helped me. He facilitated a speedy approval of my application. Once I was approved and he explained the process to me, I was shocked and grateful for his help. I did not go through the daunting process. Looking back, it was the blessing from the Lord that I decided on the right day to go and enquire, then bumped into the person I know who happened to be the executive for the housing business unit. There are no coincidences on earth. Getting a house so quickly, combined with the other things I received from the same company, made me realize how gracious and merciful God is and that his favor upon our lives is critical to cause others and systems to favor us. I felt blessed, favored and accomplished. My academic, professional, material and social areas of my life were moving in the right direction with the support of my employer. I got to travel and attend important conferences and received great training opportunities. The company not only paid my expensive student fees they also paid for my driving lessons and helped me to get my first car. The exposure I received at that company set me up for greater things later in life. I am where I am today because of the favors I had received at the onset of my career. I will forever be grateful to God, he truly makes it rain on all people, sinners and holy people, and makes the sun to shine on us all, even when we do not pay attention to him.

God loves His creation. In Proverbs 10:22 (NKJV), it says the "blessings of the Lord make one rich and are without sorrow. However, it is a sad thing for people to be showered in and with blessings on earth but die without God and go to hell. It is humbling when God's grace locates us when we are deep in sin, and the Holy Spirit helps us to open the doors of our hearts to accept God's calling into His kingdom and bring us to him so we can be with him in eternity.

WRONG FOUNDATIONS AND THE MIGHTY POWER OF GOD

God's grace and mercy are stronger than the wrong, evil foundations people are born into. In 2 Corinthians 12:9 (NKJV), the Lord says, "My grace is sufficient for you, for my strength is made perfect in weakness."

Some of the things that are brought about by foundations not established on Jesus Christ are:

Demonic influences: In my case, I believe that those evil familiar spirits knew what the Lord had in store for me and wanted to hijack the process, presenting themselves as the ones giving me blessings. This was also to fool me, so when they wanted me to serve them, they would approach in the name of the deceased maternal grandparents who came in my dreams and proclaimed I would be greatly blessed.

Those familiar spirits did try to hijack me later in life, but failed because of the grace and mercy of God. When I did not know God, Jesus Christ and the Holy Spirit, I consulted with various agents of darkness. I even went to a Buddhist temple, registered master's degree in theology, but deregistered when I realized that one of the religions to study was Islam. Though I was confused about my faith and searching for the truth, deep within my heart a voice told me to stay far away from

Islam, and I could not shake the message off. Once I deregistered master's in theology, the search continued. I tried yoga and meditation, new age positive thinking practices, read a lot of wrong books looking for God, peace and harmony in life.

The enemy, being the deceiver that he is, wanted to take advantage of my spiritual confusion and manipulate me. He tried to capture me through 3 of his evil agents I met in different settings, who told me that my ancestors, my maternal grandparents, wanted me to serve them. I was taken to these 3 agents of darkness by people closer to me, who were as lost as I was. They said I am called into the spirit realm to work for my ancestors or be a prophetess like my maternal grandmother, whom I am named after. Another even said I am called to be a witchdoctor for my ancestors.

Although I rejected this kind of calling, and was confused about my faith and spiritual life, I continued to be curious about my future, wanting to know about the unseen aspects of my life. I liked visiting a polish woman who was a well-known psychic in the city. People swore by her predictions. A friend from work told me about her and I was curious. She took me there and I got hooked. I liked talking to her about life. She seemed to know everything about the past and the future of people and countries. I thought visiting and talking with her was harmless as she was just reading cards and telling me things. I didn't know that she was consulting with familiar spirits. At her place, I saw and met a lot of professionals, businesspeople and prominent people of all walks of life, races and continents.

There was a German man who once advertised his therapeutic services, and I responded to the advert. I was going through the roughest time in my life, not knowing how to turn things around. I saw his advert as a God sent and decided to try out his services. He used hypnotherapy. He would hypnotize the clients to manipulate their brain to think and affirm positive thoughts and declare victorious statements against anything negative and evil. This too looked innocent to me. I didn't think there was anything spiritual to it. Through his tricks, I was able to breakthrough and get things back in order. I however, got concerned when he got a brain tumor and told me it is because of the brain work that he is doing for himself, presidents around the world, political parties, prominent soccer teams and many successful people to see the success and rule the world. He went to Germany for surgery. He told me a doctor and people in his organization would perform the surgery. He got comfortable with me and told me a lot of things. At times during the sessions, he would cut them short saying his forces are in and he needs to talk to them. I would not see anything or anyone around. He would rush me out, so the forces do not get upset with him for making them wait. One day he told me that he consults the same polish woman to inquire about his life. I was surprised. I don't know how he knew I also visited the same woman. He also told me that they belong to same organization and work for the same people and forces. He told me that his children who were CEOs of big companies in different countries at relatively young ages were successful because they know how to apply his therapeutic methods on themselves. He also told me though he uses his therapeutic methods for much good, he could also use it to afflict. He knew that I believed in God and wanted to plant the idea that God is not interested in our day-to-day life. We disagreed and I started having second thoughts about him for denying that God cares.

At the polish psychic woman, I also met a Jewish Architect who also called himself a light worker. One day when we were in the waiting room, we started talking about different things. He asked me to stretch out my arm so he could test my strength. At that time, I didn't know he meant spiritual strength. I did and he told me I needed balancing. He invited me to come for a session at his place. I went for a few sessions where he laid me on a massage like bed, made me relax with little light. He used some little tool to tap on different parts of the body, chanting something in a language I didn't understand. The guy was quite wealthy and lived in a rich neighborhood. His therapy office was at his house, a very beautiful house. He too told me his children were successful because they balance their lives.

These people were involved in what I came to know and understand as new age. Their practices are witchcraft practices that look harmless but very harmful in the spirit realms. There are a lot of people from all walks of life involved in such demonic practices for various reasons. There is no nation, race, country and continent spared from demonic, satanic influences. You never know the source of any person's success especially if they are not with Christ. I believe what I saw was just a tip of the iceberg.

In my search for the truth, I have encountered all sorts of agents of darkness. One of the agents of darkness even told me that my ancestors say I should stop cutting my hair. This time, I listened and decided to do dreadlocks because I didn't know how to keep my hair neat without ever cutting it. It seemed like a practical hairstyle. I did not know or understand that dreadlocks have a spiritual meaning.

The dreadlocks grew so long. I never thought anything significant about them. I just thought I happened to have long hair naturally. I didn't know the spiritual meaning of dreadlocks. I recall that I once met a lady from Nigeria who asked me if I came from the sea. That was a weird question because I had never heard that human beings could come from the ocean. What the lady said did not make sense to me. She was drawn to me in a strange way because of the long dreadlocks. She admired them. To me, it was just a hairstyle. I even forgot I kept it because an agent of darkness told me that my ancestors said I should stop cutting my hair. The lady had some sort of unusual respect and reverence for me. She told me that if I were to go to Nigeria with such long natural hair, some people would worship me because they believe any person with such long dreadlocks is from the sea. At this point, I did not know that there was a marine kingdom and marine spirits that people in darkness interact with. Once I took the dreadlocks out, instructed by the Holy Spirit to get rid of them when I became born again, I met the lady again. She was shocked that I didn't have dreadlocks anymore and could not hide her disapproval. Now, when I see anyone with dreadlocks, I wonder what their story is and why they have them.

Even before I became a born-again Christian, I started questioning whatever I heard from the agents of darkness. I believe the Lord impressed in my spirit that anything the agents of darkness were saying were lies and what we call ancestors were evil spirits, very evil with evil intention and have no love. I recall telling one agent of darkness, who told me never to cut my hair, that what she calls ancestors were evil and have no love. I said to her, if they loved people, why would they be so evil to them, asking for difficult things from people and making their lives unbearable, instilling fear and hardship if people refused to submit to them? They rule by fear and torment, which are the characteristics of evil spirits and evil deities. She was shocked to hear me say that and tried to convince me otherwise. Since that day, resentment toward anything to do with ancestors had started developing in me. Can you imagine the joy I felt when it was confirmed to me through the word of God that indeed, there are no ancestors and deceased cannot speak and demand things from the living. I knew it in my heart, without any spiritual knowledge, that something was amiss about what they called ancestors.

Considering how I came to do dreadlocks, it is no wonder the lady said what she said regarding the sea and connection to dreadlocks. I started the dreadlocks because one agent of darkness told me that my ancestors, meaning demons, say I should never cut my hair again. Dreadlocks seemed to be the most viable option to keep my hair if I were to never cut it off. I believe even the decision to choose dreadlocks was whispered into my ears by those demons, familiar spirits masquerading as ancestors. It is also interesting that once I gave my life to Christ, the first thing he told me to do was to get rid of the dreadlocks. That was the first instruction that was put in my spirit by the Holy Spirit, and I could not ignore it. I met a lady who told me that she could open up my hair and remove the dreadlocks. It took 3 days. I got rid of the dreadlocks and felt so relieved and joyful in an extraordinary way when we finished.

The dreadlocks I had were too long, and most people told me they admired them. At that time, I still did not know the spiritual meaning of dreadlocks. For a long time, I took them as just another hairstyle until I came to know after leaving the Baptist church and seeking deliverance as instructed by the Holy Spirit that they are spiritual and influenced by the marine spirits.

Mermaids, which are marine spirits, have long hair and cause people to keep dreadlocks to find expression in their lives. I am glad I am free from the spirit of dreadlocks and everything dreadlocks represented in my life. Well, ignorance is not an excuse in the spirit realm.

When a person is standing upon the wrong foundations, the enemy employs a string of wrong, evil influences to keep them in his prisons, in spiritual captivity that interferes with their physical freedom.

As I walked with the Lord, the Holy Spirit revealed the truth about such spirits and equipped me to deal with them using the word of God, the scriptures and in prayer and fasting.

It was after getting rid of the dreadlocks that I started experiencing intense spiritual attacks in my sleep for about 2 years non-stop. Without the Holy Spirit, such attacks could cause the person to lose their mind and go crazy. The attacks were heavy on my spirit, emotions and my mind. In those attacks, I saw and fought demonic beings of all kinds, such as mermaids, Satan, witches and all sorts of demons and their activities. I saw a lot of things in the spirit realm. I also used to think and believe there was no witchcraft on earth until I came to experience it firsthand, being used against me. I must say the witches that were exposed to me by the Spirit of God included people I grew up with, people I just met and people I never thought could do such things because they are highly educated and looked sophisticated in the physical realms. The Bible also made me understand that witchcraft exists, and it is a very old, demonic and evil practice. Most of the time, you cannot tell a witch by looking at a person. The Spirit of God is the one who exposes them.

I recall one of the things that happened to me after taking the dreadlocks out, and as my walk with the Lord strengthened, I fought a mermaid in my bed in the early hours of the morning. I was not completely asleep. I was just lying in bed, waiting for the sunrise. The fight was intense. I got a scratch on my arm from the fight. That was unbelievable. I defeated it. The scratch on my arm was the evidence I showed my family in the morning.

Another was in a dream, where I dreamed myself swimming in the ocean, coming out from the depths of the ocean, and different mermaid-like creatures tried to catch me without success. I managed to come out.

Another was a dream where I saw myself walking in a place that was said to be the UK, with a large body of water and a forest setting, and one street was named Satan Street. I was surprised by such a dream because I had never had such a dream and was a born-again Christian. I have also lived in the UK and never saw a street called Satan Street.

Another was a dream where three men dressed in suits, one in a light blue suit and two in dark suits, came into my bedroom the first night I prayed in tongues. Their leader said to me I needed to stop. I guess they wanted me to stop praying in tongues. I asked them who they were, and their leader dressed in a light blue suit said he was Satan. I then saw a very long light blue whip that appeared suddenly in my hand. I then lifted my hand to whip them. I said in the name of Jesus Christ and chased them away with the whip, and they ran for their lives.

In another dream, the Lord Jesus Christ was with me throughout, each time Satan appeared to come and kill me, he would see Jesus by my side. He tried 3 times and failed 3 times as the Lord Jesus was always with me. The Lord, made me understand the intensity of Satan's hatred of humans. His hatred is so deep, intense, thick and alive that you could touch it. I do not believe humans are even capable of hating like that. The Lord Jesus Christ also showed me how much he protects us from Satan's destruction until the end of our lives here on earth, and that at the end, he comes to get us. I saw myself suddenly out of the blue, healthy and strong, fall to the ground and die and immediately, raise up, and Jesus Christ was there to get me. I also saw Satan, who had been chasing my life to kill me numerous times, also appear at the end, but

Jesus Christ came first. I said to Jesus Christ, as we were walking, that the earth is a battleground. I was very happy to walk away with Jesus Christ, and Satan was watching with anger. Jesus Christ is closer to us each day than we think.

I also recall a fight with a demonic being, a familiar spirit in the image of a boy from the town I grew up, who died when I was in my youth. He wrote plays and used to be our drama leader and teacher. In the dream, the evil spirit appearing in his image was claiming me to be its wife. I fought it and overcame it, calling on the name of Jesus Christ and immediately woke up. This evil being is what people call a spirit spouse. When I woke up from that dream, I heard a clear, audible voice saying to me Read Psalm 91. I did, and immediately it was printed on the tablet of my heart, and I never forgot it to this day. The way Psalm 91 was immediately printed in my heart was a supernatural experience.

Before I took out dreadlocks, I never had such wild dreams. After taking out the dreadlocks, I frequently had dreams that would make even the worst horror movie seem mild and peaceful. I have seen things in the spirit, both good and bad, that people would generally dismiss as a conspiracy or call me a lunatic and fanatic if I were to tell my experiences. Life is more spiritual than most people care to believe. I know the power of salvation in Christ and that every knee bows at the mention of the name of Jesus Christ. The name of Jesus Christ is truly above any other name.

Talking about dead people claiming to be spouses, I also dreamed of my maternal grandfather, who was married to the grandmother I am named after. This is also the maternal grandfather who appeared in my dreams with my grandmother when I was at university campus telling me I would have lots of blessings. In this dream he looked very old and was following me around, expressively saying he wants to sleep with me as his wife. I rebuked him in the name of Jesus Christ. This was another familiar spirit presenting as a spirit spouse. In that dream, one of my cousins from my maternal side, whom I have not seen for ages and used to be very close to me when we were young, was there as if facilitating the wickedness. Spirit spouses are the work of witchcraft.

This is the same cousin whom I once saw in a vision. In the vision, she had captured me and made me her servant, as if every good thing I have serves her and I was subservient to her. She lived large in a mansion, and I was the provider of that mansion. She did not work, and I was working to provide for her and serve her. Truly, nothing is hidden from the Holy Spirit; he reveals that which is hidden. Coming to understand the things of the Spirit, I know spiritually, a person can work but never see the results of the money they earn as it gets stolen spiritually through various things such as broken car, illnesses etc. When the person has money, those incidences happen to take the money away and someone else is receive it. A person thinks that they are making a payment. The person they pay receives the money but will not account for it as spiritually the money is taken. This is how they steal money and spiritually exchange things. Spiritual exchanges happen and are complicated. Brains, money, marriages, destinies, children and many things can be exchanged spiritually.

This cousin used to be very close to me when I was growing up. One day, she called me and asked for my house number, saying her husband was coming to a conference in a city next to mine. He never came, and since giving her our address, I lost my job, started having a cat coming to my front door every morning around 9 am to cry. I eventually sold the house I had built after living in it for 1.5 years when I got another job that paid less than the salary I had when I built the house. Before I lost my job, the Holy Spirit had shown me that I would lose my job through some wicked activities done by 2 women with a closer proximity to me.

After losing that job, the Holy Spirit showed me that I would get another job. What I saw were three spiritual beings with swords coming from above. One, who seemed to be their leader, said to the two, "Go this way." They were ready to fight and were going to a battle. After this dream, I got a job in a place where I still work today. Everything I had lost has been restored. Before this, I worked in many places in different countries and the maximum period would be just two years or less in any job. But with the job that came from the Lord, I have been in the organization for over 10 years now and have been promoted a few times.

Coming back to the cousin, one night, I prayed powerful prayers to deal with astral travelers raging against us with their witchcraft. It was clear that there were evil people of darkness astral projecting and travelling to attack our lives. In the morning, I received a call from the same cousin telling me that her daughter had fallen mysteriously, her spine was broken, and she was in a hospital. By this time, I knew that my cousin was not as innocent as I used to think. I knew she liked consulting with people of darkness, but never thought she could do me wickedness. I used to trust her. The surprising thing is that she told a different story to the family. I wonder why.

Apparently, to the family, she said that the child was just sick. Since then, she stopped calling or texting me and has never called me again. Whenever I visit family in the city where she lives, she would avoid meeting me. She would promise to come and never come. I have given up on ever relating with her for as long as she is walking contrary to me spiritually. Before this, she would do anything for us to spend time together whenever I visited. It makes you wonder what has chased her away. I guess it is the power of the name of Jesus Christ, active and working in my life. I have tried to witness the gospel to her, and she responded by drifting away from me.

In Matthew 10:34-36 (NKJV), Jesus Christ said, "Do not think that I came to bring peace on the earth; I did not come to bring peace, but a sword. For I have come to 'set a man against his father, a daughter against her mother, and a daughter-in-law against her mother-in-law', and 'a man's enemies will be those of his own household." I have come to know firsthand what Jesus Christ was talking about. The name of Jesus Christ and the power of the Holy Spirit has kept me alive when some people of my household wanted me six feet under, and my immediate family completely destroyed.

Micah 7:2-6 (NKJV) says, "The faithful man has perished from the earth, and there is no one upright among men. They lie in wait for blood; every man hunts his brother with a net, that they may successfully do evil with both hands. Do not trust a friend, do not put your confidence in a companion, guard the doors of your mouth from her who lies in your bosom. For son dishonors father, daughter rises against her mother, daughter-in-law against her mother-in-law. A man's enemies are the men of his own household."

Talking about witchcraft and people closer, I had seen multiple times in my sleep, neighbors I knew growing up in my house overseas, sometimes coming to attack me or take things away from the house. Each time, I overcame them by calling on the name of Jesus Christ and the fire of the Holy Spirit and eventually, those dreams stopped.

I also saw in my dreams, such things as snakes, bears, lions, dogs, even unusual looking dogs of sizes never seen in real life, very small. In one of the dreams, the dogs were so many and could not be numbered, , in one of the streets we used going to school in the town where I grew up, not far from our home. I rebuked them in the name of Jesus Christ and was able to pass through. I saw many other strange things and places in my dreams. In another dream, the 2 snakes I saw turned into human beings, 2 ladies who were my acquaintances in the physical life. I rebuked the snakes in the name of Jesus Christ and called on the fire of the Holy Ghost to burn them. Once I said that they turned into human beings, and ran away.

In physical realms, the 2 ladies did not know each other, and both proclaimed to be Christians. I wonder why the snakes took their appearances, and they appeared together in my dream. Before this dream, the 2 ladies would call me to their gatherings and socialized very well with me. Since I saw them in the dream, they both stopped contacting me or calling me for many years now. They avoid me now. It makes you wonder what made them stop calling and inviting me to their houses and parties like they did before. Life is truly spiritual. Dreams and visions are in the spirit realm, which rules the physical realm. Victory in the spirit realm means victory in the physical realm.

I overcame all these challenges in the dreams, calling on the name of Jesus Christ and the fire of God. One time, I was half asleep and half awake. I heard a clear, audible voice saying to me, "How sure are you that you will enter heaven?" I responded, "Because of the blood of Jesus Christ," and the voice stopped.

Micah 7:7-8 (NLT) says, "As for me, I look to the LORD for help. I wait confidently for God to save me, and my God will certainly hear me. Do not gloat over me, my enemies! For though I fall, I will rise again. Though I sit in darkness, the LORD will be my light."

Micah 7:9-10 (NIV) says, "Because I have sinned against him, I will bear the LORD's wrath, until he pleads my case and upholds my cause. He will bring me out into the light; I will see his righteousness. Then my enemies will see it and will be covered with shame, she who said to me, "Where is the LORD your God?" My eyes will see her downfall, even now she will be trampled underfoot like mire in the streets." Coming into the light of God has delivered me from the hands of the wicked. The Lord has seen my shame, nakedness and sin. He pleaded my case and delivered me. I have seen the mighty hand of God. The name of Jesus Christ is powerful.

These are just some of the things I saw and experienced since I became a born-again Christian and got rid of the dreadlocks.

Through these experiences, I came to know and understand the power of the name and the blood of Jesus Christ and the Holy Spirit in the spirit realm. I overcame every evil attack in my sleep and in my waking state, calling on the name of Jesus Christ, declaring the blood of Jesus Christ and the power of the Holy Spirit. I have also allowed the Holy Spirit to lead me in the path of healing and deliverance. He has used some of his anointed servants from different parts of the world to deliver me through his word, laying on of hands and casting out evil spirits in my life. The Bible says in Philippians 2:10-11 (NKJV) that "At the name of Jesus every knee should bow, of those in heaven, and of those on earth, and of those under the earth, and that every tongue should confess that Jesus Christ is Lord, to the glory of God the Father."

I have also encountered Jesus Christ in dynamic ways during this time, seeing him, his writings and speaking to him. These experiences of the spirit realm in my sleep or half-sleep state and waking state have strengthened my faith and dependence on Jesus Christ, his blood, the Holy Spirit and the word of God, the Bible. God is truly merciful and does fight our battles, big and small, the ones we see and the ones we do not see.

Wrong covenants: In the place where I grew up, people patronized and depended on the services of the evil agents of darkness such as witchdoctors, witches, wizards, false prophets, false churches and people of that nature who used dark powers from Satan for many things such as protection, wealth, success at every level of life, casting curses and placing witchcraft on other people. When people engage, consult and look for deliverance from evil attacks and witchcraft from agents of darkness, they enter evil, ungodly covenants. Sin is the source of such covenants and the outcome of faulty, ungodly foundations that make people, even churchgoers to think darkness is the light.

Each time a person enters a place where an agent of darkness operates, such as witchdoctors, psychics, palm readers, false prophets, false churches, false Jesus/gods and deities, they submit to the altar of that place and their covenants. Those are then enforced by demons and evil spirits of that place in the lives of the patrons of that altar. In Leviticus 19:31 (ESV), it says, "Do not turn to mediums or necromancers; do not seek them out and so make yourselves unclean by them; I am the Lord your God." It also says in Leviticus 20:6 that "If a person turns to mediums and necromancers, whoring after them, I will cut him off from among my people."

Seeking help from falsehood disconnects people from God. Falsehood entails any practice that rejects Jesus Christ as the only way to God, the truth of God and the life from God.

I wonder if many people would visit the agents and places of darkness if they knew that such visits compromised them spiritually and physically. Such visits connect people to Satan, who is not interested in casting himself out of their lives, resolving any of their issues. He is only interested and specializes in giving highly superficial and temporary successes and relief to keep his victims on a leash.

Just like many, we were deceived in this way. My family visited and engaged agents of darkness, such as witchdoctors and false prophets, for protection and help with issues of life. Due to this, growing up, we were inclined to turn to those agents of darkness for various reasons, even if the family went to an Anglican church for generations and parents were actively involved in the church. There were a lot of Anglican members from the leadership to the congregants who patronized agents of darkness. The church even had witchdoctors and people who practiced abominable things, baptized and confirmed as members of the church. The church never pointed out their sin of doubling with darkness or tried to lead them to accept Jesus Christ and repent their acts.

In Acts 19, when people in Ephesus came to know about the power of God, seeing miracles and mighty works of God through Apostle Paul and the attack by the demon on the seven sons of Sceva who were not believers but used the name of Jesus Christ to cast out demons, people were filled with fear and the name of Jesus Christ was lifted high and many came to believe. It says in Acts 19:18-19 (NKJV), "And many who had believed came confessing and telling their deeds. Also, many of those who had practiced magic (sorcery, witchcraft) brought their books together and burned them in the sight of all (in public). And they counted up the value of them, and it totaled fifty thousand pieces of silver." The passage in the book of Acts indicates that any preacher who does not know Jesus Christ cannot help the lost and set them free from demonic possession using the name of Jesus Christ. It also indicates that for those who find the truth in the gospel and are delivered, they become free and renounce their evil deeds and are happy to do it publicly. It takes true salvation to confess sin in the open and expose the works of darkness. Any "Christian" church that cannot get people to repent is questionable.

As I have stated before, going to Anglican did not help us to know salvation, Jesus Christ and the Holy Spirit of the Bible. I will always wonder about the altar and covenants of the Anglican Church and what congregants sign themselves up to spiritually as members of the Anglican Church, and the covenants in operation at the church altar.

I believe a Christian church should not let tradition mix with the Bible and the gospel of Jesus Christ. People go to church to find the truth. Any church that fails to deliver people from darkness is a failed mission and undermines the true covenant of the blood of Jesus Christ. This attitude of turning a blind eye to sin can spiritually compromise congregants, offering them a highway to hell if they do not wake up and seek the truth for themselves and by the mercy and the grace of God.

Only a place of worship that 1. worships God in spirit and truth, 2. calls people to repentance, 3. acknowledges Jesus Christ of the Bible and His word and message as the only truth, the only way and the only life, 4. welcomes the Holy Spirit in His diverse forms (the gifts of the Holy Spirit) and 5. accept victory in the covenant blood of Jesus Christ, is of God. It is a place with an altar that leads to life, to heaven and eternity with God. Any place of worship that fails to do these things is dangerous and can be destructive. Be careful of the covenants in operation in places you patronize and worship at.

Seemingly innocent practices that are spiritually wrong: Some of my siblings and I were very obsessed with horoscopes and astrology. We did not know that God forbade astrology and predictions of the future. In Deuteronomy 17:2-5 it says, "If there is found among you, within your towns that the LORD your God is giving you, a man or woman who does what is evil in the sight of the LORD your God, in transgressing his covenant, and has gone and served other gods and worshipped them, or the sun or the moon or any of the hosts of heaven, which I have forbidden, and it is told you and you hear of it, then you shall inquire diligently, and if it is true and certain that such an abomination has been done in Israel, then you shall bring out to your gates that man or woman who has done this evil thing, and you shall stone that man or woman to death with stones." Engaging astrology in all its forms destroys people spiritually and physically. God says we should not defile ourselves with such practices. It is an abomination to God who created the stars. Human should look to God for guidance and not his creation.

When people follow astrology and read horoscopes, they are worshipping strange gods; they are serving Satan. 2 Kings 17:16 (ESV) says, "And they abandoned all the commandments of the LORD their God and made themselves metal images of two calves; and they made an Asherah and worshipped all hosts of heaven and served Baal." Astrology is intended to deceive people and make predictions that could mislead people. In Zechariah 10:2, it says, "For the household gods utter nonsense, and the diviners see lies; they tell false dreams and give empty consolation. Therefore, the people wander like sheep, they are afflicted for lack of a shepherd." This is also true if people go to churches and false places of worship where the truth is not taught and preached. It soothes the heart at the expense of the truth that convicts.

Astrology is the same as divination. In Isaiah 47:13-14 (NKJV), it says, "You are wearied in the multitude of your counsels; Let now the astrologers, the stargazers, and the monthly prognosticators stand up and save you from what shall come upon you. Behold, they shall be as stubble, the fire shall burn them, they shall not deliver themselves from the power of the flame, it shall not be a coal to be warmed by nor a fire to sit by."

Astrologers and predictors of the future such as psychics, just like those who practice witchcraft, are destined to the lake of fire, the unquenchable fire that never stops. They are deceivers and can never deliver themselves or anyone. They comfort itchy ears with empty predictions.

Only the name of Jesus Christ, called by those who are born-again, can deliver people. Only the Holy Spirit knows the truth and can tell born-again Christians of the things to come. No man can tell anyone of the things to come if they are not directed by God. They can guess as the familiar spirits whisper information about people to them. Telling the future and the truth is in the jurisdiction of the Holy Spirit. As stated in John 16:13 (NKJV), "However, when he, the Spirit of truth, has come, he will guide you into all truth; for he will not speak on his own authority, but whatever he hears he will speak, and he will tell you things to come." It means that only the Holy Spirit, who was here on earth at the beginning of time and is still here, knows the truth and can tell it to born-again believers. Other means to tell the future and predict what is to come are the schemes of the devil.

We didn't know that any means of prediction of the future and astrology are falsehood. We even had a horoscope book that detailed every star sign. We believed what the book said and thought it was an innocent book to help people define and understand themselves and others, and it was not a sin. We literally analyzed ourselves and others based on star signs. It was a guidebook so we thought. The book was addictive. Now I know it was spiritual and nothing innocent about it. This book was an abomination to God and reading it was an abominable deed before God. The book is like Satan presenting himself as an angel of light. These are the kinds of books the lost read and draw hope from, even though they never help anyone. They are new-age tools promoting philosophies and ideologies that encourage self-help and self-dependence instead of looking to God for guidance through His Word and by His Spirit.

I was sort of addicted to reading everything about horoscopes. I religiously read the daily horoscopes in the newspaper for a very long time and relied on their predictions for my daily outlook. At that time, I thought this was just normal life. The reality is that nothing that was predicted ever manifested in my life. However, the addiction to reading the horoscopes was deep and undeniable. The practice seemed so innocent, harmless and nothing dangerous. I liken this to a situation where someone uses recreational marijuana and thinks it is harmless, and the next thing they know, they are addicted to heavy drugs. Reading horoscopes and predictions about life is so addictive that it is easy to fall deep into it and make it the main source of truth about the deep things of life and even end up getting into the occult. It is very dangerous. It is like a carrot that is dangling and you keep on reaching out to try and get it. Horoscopes entice the prey to keep coming for more.

In Daniel 2:27-28, it says, "No wise men, enchanters, magicians, or astrologers can show the king the mystery the king has asked, but there is God in heaven who reveals mysteries." This clearly indicates that, besides God, no spirit or man can tell the mysteries of life or accurately unpack the future. Only the Spirit of God can tell the mysteries to those who put their trust in God.

Micah 5:12, it says, "And I will cut off sorceries from your hand, and you shall have no more tellers of fortune." This is good news because God is more than able to set people free from the hold of the spirit of astrology and divination. I am free from this today. God delivered me from this before I became a born-again Christian. I just lost interest and stopped reading them, realizing they were always false and vague. They did not make sense. God can end evil influences in a place and in people, even when they are still walking far from him spiritually and physically. His grace and mercy are abundant even to the sinners.

I came to know after receiving Christ Jesus and reading the Bible for myself, about the dangers of reading and believing horoscopes and astrology. These acts separate people from God and bring affliction in the lives of people. The obsession with horoscopes and astrology was the result of faulty foundations upon which I stood from birth until I was born-again and was made new in Christ.

Things like horoscopes and astrology are New Age practices that connect people to the deceiving spirits of the devil. I also remember we thought dead relatives were somehow connected to the living and were closer to God and brought messages from God to the living. Reading horoscopes was a deception about messages from another world and the future.

Before I became a Christian, I also watched some programs on TV where a medium was telling people on the show what their dead relatives were saying. This was purely a necromancy program, evil presented as good. I did not know that a medium was being told what to say by evil spirits called familiar spirits connected to families of those who attended the show. The funny thing was that the programs were international. The mediums were males and females attending to people of diverse races, backgrounds, and economic status. I imagine most people attended such shows innocently, desperate to hear from the other world, and thinking there was no harm in doing that. I bet they did not know that such shows opened them to demonic manipulations and attacks. This goes to show that throughout the world, there are a lot of lost souls, and that the devils prey on unsuspecting victims in similar ways despite their origin, color or continent.

The interesting thing is that I would often feel a bit scared, unsettling presence and fearful whenever I watched that program. Something within me knew there was something unclean about those TV shows. However, I continued watching because I was fascinated and intrigued that people could hear from their dead relatives. Life after death is a mystery, especially when you don't have Christ. The program brought a mingling of comfort about the deceased and fear at the same time. An important question is asked in Isaiah 8:19 that says, "Why consult the dead-on behalf of the living?"

Jesus Christ is the only truth, and the testimony of Jesus Christ is the spirit of prophecy (Revelation 19:10) and dispels all the lies of the enemy. Jesus Christ is the only light and his testimony exposes the deception of the enemy and uncovers darkness wherever it is hiding. Jesus Christ is the only way that connects people to what is real in the spiritual realm.

The Bible says deception and fear are of the devil. Whatever messages the people heard from those TV shows were deceptions by masquerading familiar spirits disguised as people's loved ones. It is interesting that the world over, people want a connection with the spirit realm, even if it is their deceased relatives. The desire for a spiritual connection through wrong means makes people a low-hanging fruit for the devil, the father of lies. Human beings are spirits clothed in mortal bodies. That is why there is a deep longing in any person for a spiritual connection with higher realms than earth and curiosity about the unseen world. A human soul knows that there is power higher than itself, beyond human ability, existence and comprehension. The only concerning thing is that Satan has managed to capitalize on this spiritual side of humanity to deceive humanity in various ways.

There was also a TV program that talked about people's experiences of heaven, hell, demonic encounters and Jesus Christ. I could never get myself to watch this program. It scared me so much, even more than the necromancy program. It boils down to the erroneous foundation away from the true Jesus Christ. Now that I am saved by God's grace, born again by the Spirit of God, I have stopped watching evil programs about necromancy and related subjects. I now watch testimonies of heaven and hell, spiritual encounters of all kinds, miracles, signs and wonders of the supernatural realms from other Christians with curiosity and peace. Each time I watch testimonies of born-again Christian , I feel humbled, loved and blessed by God to have been saved by His grace. Salvation in Christ is truly a humbling gift that only God can give and is received by faith.

Doctrines of demons: I was really lost with lack of knowledge of the scriptures and having my own twisted perception and understanding of God, Jesus Christ and the Holy Spirit drawn from heresy. The Bible calls that twisted perspective "the doctrine of demons." The doctrine I had received in my youth did not help or empower me spiritually. I was in a serious spiritual deficit and stumbled in my decisions and choices until the Holy Spirit, the Spirit of truth, led me into all truth. It says in 1 Timothy 4:1-2 (NKJV and NIV) that "Now the Spirit says that in the latter times some will depart from the faith, giving heed to deceiving spirits and doctrines of demons. Such teachings come through hypocritical liars, whose consciences have been seared as with a hot iron."

The Bible also says in Hosea 4: (NKJV) that "My people are destroyed for lack of knowledge. Because you have rejected knowledge, I will reject you from being priests for me; because you have forgotten the law of your God, I also will forget your children." This indicates that being lost and living far from God is a generational issue because those who came before failed to follow God. A generation that rejects God creates a pathway for the devil to deceive the next generations. This is the reason the world is filled with doctrines that are unbiblical and a buffet of religious practice to choose from.

Exposure to erroneous doctrines outside the Bible causes people to stumble. The world is filled with and foiled by religions and spiritual practices founded upon the doctrines of demons. Some of the founders of false religions claim they had visitations of angels or spiritual beings who gave them messages, and they started their religious movements afterwards. Those spiritual beings or angels were evil spirits and demons who are to this day bent on getting humanity to think there are many ways to God. These evil spirits are so cruel that they even get some people to worship trees, stones, the water, the sun, the moon and the dead, even dead gurus, saints or prophets as their gods or mediators to the true God. They give their followers a twisted doctrine. Most of the false practices have some flavor of Christianity and the Bible while at the same time opposing it because the devils know that the Bible holds the truth and that Jesus Christ is the only way and the only mediator between God and man. 1 Timothy 2:5 (NKJV) says, "For there is one God and one Mediator between God and men, the Man Christ Jesus."

Any religion without Jesus Christ of the Bible as the focal point is from Satan, serves and worships devils. Doctrines of demons establish wrong, broken foundations in people's lives because it does not establish Jesus Christ as their foundation. Psalm 11:3 says, "If the foundations are destroyed, what can the righteous do?" Doctrine of demons could include words that sound spiritual and holy but are just twisted truths to capture the souls of devoted unsuspecting congregants, praying to wrong gods and idols using various items and means such as yoga, meditations, saints, figurines, false deities, invoking spirits of dead saints, and bowing to statues and evil altars even if it is in a church or any place of worship, creating a broken spiritual foundation which then influence people's choices, deeds, opinions and perspectives of life.

Demons give their doctrines to deceive people and use what people call spiritual, church, place of worship or a person of God, false priests to propagate their deception and keep people in darkness. The doctrine of demons in their various forms are very dangerous and meant to permanently separate humanity from God, who created them out of love. These doctrines of demons indicate that on earth, there is a perpetual fight and battle for human souls in the spirit realms. When you live away from God, Jesus Christ and the Holy Spirit, you become a child of darkness. The night becomes your cover. Following the wrong religion is akin to being perpetually asleep spiritually, even if you are physically awake. Sleep is of the night and darkness. Those doctrines of demons keep people and nations in darkness for generations.

In 1 Thessalonians 5:5-6 (NKJV), Christians are reminded that "You are all sons of the light and the sons of day. We are not of the night nor of darkness. Therefore, let us not sleep as others do; but let us watch and be sober."

The Bible says the children of God are the children of the light and the children of the day, and are always awake spiritually. Jesus Christ is their light, and in him there is no night or darkness; it is only day and life.1 John 1:5 (NKJV) says, "This is the message which we have heard from Him and declare to you, that God is light and in Him is no darkness at all." Following Jesus Christ is also a generational issue. The generation that chooses God creates a pathway for God's blessings and preservation for generations to come. Psalm 37:28 (NKJV) says, "For the LORD loves justice and does not forsake his saints; they are preserved forever; but the descendants (seed, children) of the wicked shall be cut off."

The light of God is the gift of God to His children. James 1:16-17 (NKJV) says, "Do not be deceived, my beloved brothers and sisters.

Every good gift and every perfect gift is from above, and comes down from the Father of lights, with whom there is not variation or shifting shadow."

Those who are with the true living God, saved by grace through the blood of Jesus Christ, are the children of the light and of the day. Hallelujah to the one in whom there is no darkness and preserves his saints and their seed for generations.

Demonic and witchcraft operations: Another evidence of faulty foundations is a person and a place that attracts evil things and experiences. Where there is witchcraft and presence of demonic powers and entities, there is lawlessness Also places that are filled and littered with visible or invisible uncleanliness including such things as unkept appearances, cockroaches, ants, bed bugs, lizards, scorpions, rats that are unmanageable and unruly, creepy crawling creatures and things running in the roof of the house, scorpions, snakes and dangerous creatures in unexpected places are signs of demonic and witchcraft foundations. Foundations built upon covenants at evil altars attract demonic operations and witchcraft in the lives of people. Their operations communicate the spiritual uncleanliness of the place and of the people in that place. The blood of Jesus Christ cleanses people and places from demonic and witchcraft operations and brings them liberty.

Wrong people and evil altars: It was only after giving my life to Jesus Christ and learned about the spiritual realm that I came to realize that life outside the altar of the cross of Jesus Christ is dangerous and is generally lived on evil altars. Evil altars are spiritual platforms and powers used by those who are not using the altar of the cross of Jesus Christ for their spiritual lives to maneuver and manipulate life, and a launchpad into spiritual environments. The spirits behind evil altars that manifest the outcomes for those who use evil altars are demons and evil spirits. Remember, Satan is an evil spirit and a devil. These spirits work through evil altars and covenants established at those evil altars in various ways and means.

The world is filled with practitioners of evil altars who are continuously forging evil covenants with unsuspecting individuals looking for answers to the issue of life in the wrong places. They also use those evil altars and covenants to hurt and destroy people's lives. I was a victim of these and was too blind spiritually to identify the wrong people belonging to evil altars. I have met too many seemingly good people willing to offer help from the wrong places with demonic altars. There are also plenty of books to read that keep people on the broad road that leads to destruction. Satan uses and enforces his plans using people, books, movies, songs, games and many other things in the world to ensure the evil altars and covenants are kept alive for generations.

When a person visits wrong places, including those that are socially accepted like pubs, spiritual healing places, wild parties, carnal or demonic festivals, events such as Halloween and demonic concerts, false places of worship and prayer, ritual places, that person goes to an altar and enters demonic, evil covenants with the spirits of those altars. Imagine if a person goes to many of those diverse places. This is how the enemy captures people as he deceives and influences their life choices.

The thing is, when you visit such places and agree with their offers, you become highly compromised spiritually. When those wrong people and places fall, you fall with them. This is the reason everyone needs deliverance. Today, it's easy to be a victim of those evil people and places, as many things and practices have been normalized, and people are desensitized to accepting evil as good. In Isaiah 31:1-3 (NKJV), it says, "Woe to those who go down to Egypt for help, and rely on horses, who trust in chariots because there are many, and in horsemen because they are very strong, but who do not look to the Holy One of Israel, nor seek the LORD! Yet He also is wise and will bring disaster, and will not call back His words, but will arise against the house of evildoers, and against the help of those who work iniquity. Now the Egyptians are men, and not God, and their horses are flesh, and not spirit. When the

LORD stretches out His hand, both he who helps will fall, and he who is helped will fall down, they all will perish together."

Isaiah 48:22 (NKJV) says, "There is no peace," says the LORD, "for the wicked." This is true. People who live far from God, Jesus Christ and His Spirit never have peace. They may numb their lack of peace by keeping busy with many things or engaging in many destructive behaviors. 1 Corinthians 14:33 (NKJV) says, "For God is not the author of confusion but of peace, as in all the churches of the saints." Peace is only found in Jesus Christ, the Prince of Peace. And only the Word of God and the Holy Spirit are qualified to lead people in the right paths, eliminating the need for wrong people and evil altars.

Many of the elements that create wrong foundations stem from the acts of the flesh.

THE ACTS OF THE FLESH, THE DEVIL'S CARROT: GALATIANS 5:19-21

The world has a way of giving people false comfort and unstable blessings because they are not built upon the firm foundation that only God gives. The Bible in Proverbs 10:22 (NKJV) says, "The blessing of the LORD makes one rich, and he adds no sorrow with it."

Many people are driven to achieve outward success rather than inner integrity. The material life and its glitz and glamour never cease to entice people to want more of the outward display of accomplishments. Some people will do anything to get whatever they want, despite the costs.

The spirit within might be screaming no, hold on, not now, wait, and at the same time, another voice within might be saying the opposite. This is because in life, there is constant conflict between the spirit of God (the Holy Spirit) and the human flesh (the sinful nature of man) that seeks attention, power, control, status, riches and dominion. The spirit in every person comes from God, belongs to God and knows what is best for each person at any given time. However, the person is made up of the soul, the spirit and the mind. The person's soul and mind belong to them, and every person is in control of their own soul and mind. Even the Bible cautions about this when Jesus Christ says in Mark 8:36-37 (KJV) "For what shall it profit a man, if he shall gain the whole world, and lose his own soul? Or what shall a man give in exchange for his soul?"

The works of the flesh, as stated in the Bible, are the reasons people trade their souls to gain the world. Some people who are disconnected from God can never hear the voice of the spirit within them because the flesh has taken over. Their souls and minds are in control and drive them to want gratification at every level. The Maslow hierarchy of needs is a good example of how the flesh rules in the lives of people. From the basic to the highest level on needs, the self takes the center stage. It is all about self-actualization and gratification without God.

Paul writes in Galatians 5:19-21 (NKJV), "Now the works of the flesh are evident, which are: adultery, fornication, uncleanness, lewdness, idolatry, sorcery, enmities/hatred, contentions/strife, jealousies, outburst of wrath, selfish ambitions, dissensions, heresies, envy, murders, drunkenness, revelries and the like; of which I told you beforehand, just as I also told you in time past, that those who practice such things will not inherit the kingdom of God."

Adultery, evidenced by the rate of divorces around the world due to unfaithfulness in marriage or fake marriages for various reasons, such as to gain money in exchange of citizenship or opportunities, etc.

Fornication, meaning sexual relations between unmarried people, including prostitution. This is a rife, pervasive practice around the world which is responsible for many related afflictions and sins like masturbation, nudity, child pornography, sexual molestations, and pornography at large, single and youth parenthood, sexually transmitted diseases and many other unholy acts even among the young children in this day and age of technology.

Uncleanness, this can be in the spirit and/or in the physical form with our bodies, hearts, minds, words, thoughts and environments.

Lasciviousness, meaning homosexuality, including transgenderism and supporting pronouns, has become a socially accepted practice in many countries. The acceptance of this abomination has even penetrated some churches, where pastors are willing to marry same sex partners or themselves are homosexuals in the church to encourage acceptance in the broader society, and education systems where such is openly discussed in schools with students of all ages as part of sex education. Some washrooms have become gender neutral and there are legislations and regulations protecting this abomination. Those who openly oppose are generally faced with the likelihood of a jail time. In some countries, some parts of the bible such as Galatians 5, Leviticus 18:22, 20:13, Deuteronomy 23:18, Romans 1:27, 1 Corinthians 6:9, 1 Timothy 1:10, Revelation 21:8 are considered hate speech because they address lasciviousness directly. Some pastors shy away from preaching and teaching about these parts of the bible to play safe and avoid persecution. Jesus did not promise Christinas an easy time on earth. He said persecution would come and if they hated him they would hate those who are his disciples.

Idolatry/sorcery/iniquity, meaning anything that takes priority in our lives over God, and exalts itself above the knowledge of God, forming strongholds in the lives of people, families and nations.

In the Bible, stubbornness is put in the same category as idolatry, sorcery and iniquity. This is interesting because generally people do not think much about their stubborn attitudes. It means there are a lot of idolaters and sorcerers in the world because their stubborn attitudes qualify them as such.

Whatever comes before God in a person's life, and that can be as innocent as a wife, husband, children, friends, family, job or business, those things have become idols, gods and objects of worship. Idolatry is a stronghold. The Bible says strongholds of any kind must be pulled down. In this day and age, there are enough things to take away our attention from the Lord and become idols. People do not have to try harder. The advent of the internet has transformed lives and continues to transform things. Now humanity is even faced with robots and

Artificial Intelligence (AI) that seem to be smarter than some people. Soon, these will become entrenched in many people's lives to the extent that they will not know how to function without the help of robots and AI. Unchecked, robots and AI would become the masters of humanity, idols they hold dear. I can imagine in the future some churches using robotic AI to deliver sermons, give counselling to humans and many other things. This would truly be an abomination to the Lord. People have many things they hold dear in their imaginations and hearts, other than God. Just excessive use and adoration of cellphones, social media, technology, sports tournaments, celebrities, and many other things have captured the hearts, souls and minds of many and therefore have become man-made gods and objects of worship.

Witchcraft and this includes, according to the Bible, the spirit of rebellion (1 Samuel 15:23) and related spirits. Considering how many people are rebellious, many practice witchcraft unknowingly. Some think that they are doing the right thing when they rebel and demonstrate in the streets against unfair practices, laws, and oppression. Such are sometimes done with good intentions in the eyes of man, but separate people from God. Sometimes, demonstrations do turn violent and in opposition to the will of God for men. The Bible recommends peaceful resolutions.

Hatred, I believe, many wars and disgraceful, vicious acts on earth are the product of hatred. Hate has escalated around the world, and many are open about their views, even if their views are hateful. The only thing humanity should hate is sin. Hating sin helps to keep people obedient to God and righteous before God. The bible says righteousness exalts the nation. Righteousness can exalt individuals, families and communities. We ought not to hate anyone, even if we do not approve of them. Hate is the opposite of love, compassion, mercy and grace and blinds people to what is good. A hateful heart is an unloving, uncompassionate and merciless heart.

Variances, meaning active, persistent disagreements, arguments, debates or differing views that cause people to hate each other. Unchecked, this can become a very common occurrence even amongst people who claim to love each other. Variances that result in conflict instead of peace are evil.

Emulations, meaning observed jealousy and contentious rivalry, which could include competition. Emulations are everywhere, in families, workplaces, churches, society, world governments, business world. The competitive nature of life has given birth to emulations. This is old since the time of Adam. Cain was jealous of Abel and ended up killing Abel.

Wrath, meaning intense anger. Anger is not a sin if the person recognizes it, repents of it and forgives. Sometimes anger drives people to reject that which is evil and desire that which is noble and good. Wrath is unrepentant anger that seeks to avenge, to hurt, inflict pain and destroy.

Strife, meaning a bitter clash or quarrel normally resulting in unforgiveness and offence, is found in many places and has caused many wars, disagreements and many other related responses among people, friends, families, nations and even in the churches.

Sedition, meaning revolting against lawful authorities. The history of many nations is filled with acts of sedition. Sedition is closely related to rebellion. In the Bible, when the children of Israel left Egypt with Moses as their lawful authority, those who rebelled against him were punished by the Lord. When his brother Aaron and sister Mariam rebelled against him taking a foreign wife, Mariam was smitten with leprosy. Again, when Korah and his followers rebelled against Moses and Aaron as their lawful authorities, it says in Numbers 16:32 that "and the earth opened its mouth and swallowed them up, with their households and all the men with Korah, with all their goods." In the Bible, rebellion is the spirit of witchcraft.

Heresies, meaning false doctrine, doctrine of man and not of God, and religious cults. These have become a common phenomenon these days, where people's ears are itchier and find comfort in the doctrine that makes them feel good, and sin is ignored and tolerated. It is not commonplace these days to find ministers in the church willing to preach and teach about repentance and hell, as well as against sin and the consequences of sin. They teach mainly about God as the loving Father and not as a judge. They teach more of the doctrine of grace without balancing it with the whole counsel of God. This is the reason that sin and many unbiblical practices are now found in the church, accepted and accommodated among some conventional and modern churches. Convicting talks about sin, deliverance, hell, God as a loving Father and a judge from a biblical perspective are typically frowned upon. These kinds of talks are avoided in the name of making Christianity unoffensive, equal to all the other religions of the world (one world religion that claims that all religions lead to God and heaven) and acceptable to sinners.

Envying, meaning desiring that which belongs to someone else, intense jealousy for another or a resentful, dissatisfied longing for another's possession. This is closely related to emulations.

Murder. In many countries, abortion is legal and protected by the law, which causes many who are ignorant of the word of God to see no harm in this practice and encourage and perform it.

Killings of all kinds have skyrocketed the world over, with wars, terror attacks and suicide bombings becoming commonplace on top of homicide and fatal accidents.

Drunkenness, although this is mainly through alcohol, drugs, opioids and substance abuse, has increased even among the youth and the poor in many parts of the world. Drunkenness leads to addictions, which have become a menace and nuisance in many countries. Some rich nations have even legalized marijuana for tax purposes. Although this has increased government revenues, it has made the drug problem worse. The consequences of such legalizations have been devastating. There are more youth being killed by opioids and lives destroyed to the point of no return.

Drunkenness is an ancient problem. In the Bible, Genesis 19:31-38, Lot's two daughters got him drunk so they could sleep with him to bear his children because they thought no man will ever see them in the cave where they lived after Sodom and Gomorrah were destroyed through fire by God for their iniquities. In a drunken state, a person is not able to make good judgment. Lot didn't even know he had slept with his daughters. Lot's daughters produced the Moabites and the Ammonites, who became the arch enemies of the children of Israel. Anything born out of drunkenness can never be holy. Drunkenness can make a person miss the kingdom of God. This is revealed in 1 Corinthians 6:9-10 (NKJV) that says drunkards are among those who will not inherit the kingdom of God. Alcohol drinking is a commonly accepted social practice around the world, and its dangers are sometimes overlooked and escalated by the use and abuse of drugs and other substances that are taking many lives around the world.

Reveling and related acts, meaning loud, noisy, disorderly, wild parties, feasts, concerts and festivals, bars, drinking parlors and many such places, which are accepted as social platforms around the world. Many people find pleasure in such gatherings and label them as fun.

The interesting thing is that all these acts of the flesh relate back to the things the Lord God commanded humanity not to do in the 10 commandments, written and given to Moses by God on Mount Sinai.

Looking closely at the acts of the flesh, one can see the devil, Satan, the ancient serpent written all over. Every act of the flesh is a character of the devil. It is true that the devil is the father of the acts of the flesh and entices people of all ages to engage with one or more of these without repenting for generations, so he can have a strong foothold in people's lives. It is not uncommon to find a selfish child. This is because we live in a fallen world that worships the flesh and makes it easy for the devil to access the people with the intention to subvert the purposes of God on earth.

Though the acts of the flesh are expressed physically for all to see, their root cause is spiritual in nature. In this fallen world, the acts of the flesh are ruling and running rampant in the lives of the people. Life at the flesh level is sanctioned by systems that promote woke culture in societies today. The acts of the flesh have become accepted as normal life in many parts of the world.

Without the Holy Spirit, it is hard to detect what is holy and what is unholy, what is of the flesh and what is of God. An antidote to the acts of the flesh is the Fruit of the Holy Spirit. A person needs the whole Fruit of the Holy Spirit to overcome just one act of the flesh. This indicates that each act of the flesh can become a stronghold on its own. I believe behind each act of the flesh, there is a demon, an evil spirit, sometimes multiple, feeding off that act each time the host engages in the act.

Engaging in and taking comfort in the acts of the flesh is not worth it. It is short-sightedness because this life will end for everyone, and we will all have to face God for judgment. The Bible says in 1 Corinthians 6:9-10 (NKJV) "Do you not know that the unrighteous will not inherit the kingdom of God? Do not be deceived. Neither fornicators, nor idolaters, nor adulterers, nor homosexuals, nor sodomites, nor thieves, nor covetous, nor drunkards, nor revilers, nor extortioners will inherit the kingdom of God." The main way out of the destruction of the acts of the flesh is to walk in and be led by the Spirit of the living God in everything. This is why the Bible says "Pray without ceasing and bring everything to God in prayer and supplication with thanksgiving." In Philippians 4:6 (NKJV) it says, "Be anxious for nothing, but in everything by prayer and supplication, with thanksgiving, let your request be made known to God."

THE SPIRITUAL NATURE OF THE ACTS OF THE FLESH:

Adultery: This is a spirit that seeks to possess and influence people to violate the sacredness of marriage between man and woman. There are more divorces today because of adultery throughout the world. It is not uncommon even for Christian to divorce due to adultery. One of the commandments given by God in Exodus 20:14 says, "You shall not commit adultery." In biblical terms, adultery refers to the act of engaging in sexual relations with someone who is not one's spouse.

154

Some people commit adultery due to their inability to commit to one person, or due to curses in their families. Adultery is a spirit.

The book of Proverbs 9:17 talks about "stolen waters." The world over is filled with acts of immoralities, husbands cheating on wives and wives cheating on husbands, stolen waters. This happens even is some churches including between pastors and their congregation. This is not so frowned upon these days than before. The entertainment world has made adultery look glamorous and acceptable.

Adultery is against the will and the purposes of God when he created marriage between man and woman. In Genesis 2:24 (NKJV) God said about Adam and Eve that "Therefore a man shall leave his father and his mother, and be joined to his wife, and they shall become one flesh."

In Matthew 19:3-8 (NKJV), when the Pharisees approached Jesus Christ deceitfully and connivingly, asking him "Is it lawful for a man to divorce his wife for just reason?" Jesus said to them "Have you not read that He who made them at the beginning made them male and female, for this reason a man shall leave his father and mother and be joined to his wife, and the two shall become one flesh?," so then they are no longer two but one flesh. Therefore, what God has joined together, let not man separate."

They continued to ask him "Why then did Moses command to give a certificate of divorce, and to put her away?" Jesus answered them and said "Moses, because of the hardness of your hearts, permitted you to divorce your wives, but from the beginning it was not so. And I also say to you, whoever divorces his wife except for sexual immorality, and marries another, commits adultery, and whoever marries he who is divorced commits adultery."

This sacred union of marriage is the same as between a born again Christian and Jesus Christ. Here, I am talking about marriage that is rooted in genuine love and not any other thing. This kind of union is extrapolated in Ephesians 5:31-32 (NKJV) that says, "For this reason a man shall leave his father and mother and be joined to his wife, and the two shall become one flesh." This marriage between husband and wife symbolizes the sacred relationship between Jesus Christ and his church, the born-again Christians who are the church and the body of Christ. Christ, just as the husband is the head of the house, he is the head of the church and born-again Christians are the body, the wife of Christ. When a person becomes born-again, they become one with Christ. When a born-again Christian looks to other things to worship, they commit adultery against Jesus Christ. Born again Christians cannot worship saints or any other person, living or dead.

The church without Jesus Christ does not exist just as a person claiming to be Christian but is not born again is not a church of Christ and therefore does not belong the Jesus Christ of the Bible. Just like a woman who cohabits with a man is not married and cannot be called the wife of that man, church goers who are not born again are not the bride of Christ and therefore not one with Jesus Christ. This is what religion does. It is a sin for a woman to cohabit with a man just like it is a sin to reject salvation through Christ alone. The person might belong to another Jesus who is not the Christ of the Bible. It is written that many false Christs shall come and declare themselves the Christ and many shall follow them.

Adultery is not only limited to the physical realm and between human beings. It also applies to the spiritual realm. It is a sin of adultery to mix Jesus Christ with any other spiritual and religious customs and traditions to boost one's spiritual and physical life. As clearly articulated in Hosea 4:12-13 (BSB and NIV), looking to other things for help other than to God is a spiritual adultery and it says, "My people consult their wooden idols, and their divining rods inform them. For a spirit of prostitution leads them astray and they have played a harlot against their God. They sacrifice on the mountaintops and burn offerings on the hill, under oaks, poplars and terebinths, where the shade is pleasant. Therefore, your daughters turn to prostitution and your daughter-in-law to adultery." This indicates that the adultery parents commit against God, can affect their children and future generations. God is a generational God.

When parents commit spiritual adultery, the curse of adultery enter their households, and their children become spiritual prostitutes. This sin and curse of spiritual adultery can even be at the nation level. In Jeremiah 3:9 "Because of the indecency of her unfaithfulness, Israel defiled the land and committed adultery with stones and trees" This is also the case where there is fornication.

Fornication: This is a spirit that seeks to possess and influence people to commit sexual immorality and relations outside the boundaries of marriage and defile themselves. It is the spirit behind such things as homosexuality, transgenderism, unconventional pronouns, and many spirited lives. Fornication equates to sexual immorality. In biblical terms, it refers to illicit sexual relation outside the covenant of marriage. This sin has become so pervasive that it is an unwritten standard in many cultures. Sexual relations before marriage between partners is common and generally accepted. This sin has become normalized.

It is the spirit that is behind legalization of homosexuality in many nations and all other acts that go with it such as pride parade. Some people fornicate for survival, to get money, favor or keep their jobs. Some fornicate due to peer or family pressure, for fun, social acceptance, and to satisfy their unquenchable appetites. Some fornicate due to curses in their families.

Fornication is a spirit that comes about because people or families rejected God and his saving grace. Even Christians who reject God and his ways in their hearts find themselves battling the spirit of fornication more intensely. Because it is a spirit, it needs to be resisted spiritually so it does not gain power or launch its destructive pattern in the lives of people and families.

Some of the unrelated destructive patterns of the spirit of fornication that people see in their families include kids choosing to be transgender or homosexuals, children born outside wedlock, gender confusion, cohabitation, customary marriages, and multiple sexual partners. The enemy afflicts with such curses because the spirit of fornication has been given hold, access and a leeway into people's lives and families.

Once it gains a hold, it replicates itself to make it difficult for the people in that family to overcome its power. It becomes a stronghold in the lives of people.

The Bible tells us that the antidote for fornication is 1. To flee from it because it is not like any other sin, 2. Maintain a life of holiness and 3. Having self-control. It is the only sin that people commit against their own bodies. 1 Corinthians 6:18 says, "Flee from sexual immorality. Every other sin a man commits is outside his body, but he who sins sexually sins against his own

body." Fleeing from fornication means doing everything to stay away and out of it. One may have to refuse some social or business engagements, offers, friendships or watching compromising programs.

The antidote for stronghold is the Word of God, which is the sword in the spirit realm. The Word of God is a powerful weapon that helps born-again Christians to challenge the spirit of fornication. 2 Corinthians 10:4 (NKJV) says, "For the weapons of our warfare are not carnal, but mighty through God to pulling down of strongholds." In Hebrew 4:12 (KJV) it says, "For the word of God is quick and powerful, and sharper than any two-edged sword, piercing even to the dividing asunder of soul and spirit, and of the joints and marrow, and is a discerner of the thoughts and intense of the heart."

Fornication is the only sin a person commits against themselves. It is like a spiritual suicide, self-poisoning and self-destructive weapon. Having the Fruit of the Holy Spirit and the Word of God in the heart help to disempower the spirit of fornication. When fornication or the thoughts thereof rear their own ugly head, it is important to proclaim and declare the promises of God written in the word of God against such thoughts and desires. At times, a person may need to declare and decree the word of God multiple times before the spirit of fornication abates. God said he sent forth his word to heal and deliver his people. In Psalm 107:20 (NKJV) it says, "He sent His Word and healed them, and deliver them from their destructions." It is important to remember that Jesus Christ is the living Word of God sent to heal and deliver those who believe. The written word of God is the revelation of Jesus Christ. When the spirit of fornication is too intense in a person's life or family, a deliverance through the anointed servant of God to cast out the spirit in the name of Jesus Christ is critical.

Uncleanness: This is the spirit that seeks to possess and influence people to stay in unclean environments at every level. Uncleanness can be at the physical or spiritual level or both. It can also refer to moral and spiritual impurities, separation from God, sickness and death. That is, anything that defiles a person. Evil spirits that possessed people are unclean spirits and defile their hosts. Jesus Christ delivered many people that were tormented by unclean spirits. In the book of Acts Paul delivered a girl who had unclean spirits and was a diviner making her masters' lots of money through divination, which is witchcraft. The spirit of divination was an unclean spirit in her.

Uncleanness is a sin found in both the Old and the New Testament. Every kind of sin make people unclean. Even the land or location where people commit sin, becomes unclean.

Uncleanness is removed by the blood of a clean sacrifice. The Bible says there is no remission of sin without the shedding of the blood. The blood of Jesus Christ cleanses people and nations from all uncleanness.

In the Old Testament, people had to bring various sacrifices without blemish to the priests to remove uncleanness and basically transfer their uncleanness to the object of the sacrifice in exchange of cleanness and forgiveness of sin. In the Old Testament, this process was unending. It is more like in the lives of those who are without Christ today. They turn to many things to make their lives clean, and the process is never ending because nothing can take away sin and uncleanness without the shedding of the blood of the perfect sacrifice.

In the Old Testament, the blood of animals was never enough to remove all uncleanness. This is because the animals, even if it was without blemish, were created creatures, and conceived though mutation between male and female animals. They could never be enough to clean sin and takeaway uncleanness from the person forever.

All these acts of sacrifices where pointing to the upcoming last sacrifice that Jesus Christ offered through his life. Because Jesus Christ is God who created all things, born, died and rose again without sin, the shedding of His blood cleanses people who put their trust in him. His blood shed on the day he was crucified has given humanity a permanent sacrifice and remains effective forever. No other sacrifice is required anymore. Jesus Christ and His blood are the ultimate sacrifice to redeem people from all uncleanness.

When Jesus Christ came and went to the cross of Calvary, shedding his pure blood was for the remission of sins and to remove all uncleanness from people. He exchanged believers' uncleanness for his cleanness and sin for righteousness. All that people need to do is to receive his sacrifice by faith and turn away from all the temptations of uncleanness. On top of the blood of Jesus Christ, God has also given believers the Holy Spirit, the Spirit of the living God given by Christ Jesus, and His written Word, the Bible, to help them remain clean.

The blood of Jesus Christ that cleanse believers from all unrighteousness, gives believers access to the presence of the Lord, the throne of God, which is the Holy of Holies. The presence of the Lord is holy ground. This was clearly expressed in Exodus 3:2 (NKJV) when Moses saw the bush burning but not consumed and he decided to go close to see the strange thing he was observing. From the burning bush, a voice came out calling Moses by name and warned him not to come close, saying "Do not draw near this place. Take your sandals off your feet, for the place where you stand is holy ground."

The adversary of mankind, Satan, uses the physical and spiritual uncleanness to accuse people before God. Spiritual uncleanness can arise from a multitude of sins, transgressions and abominable things practiced by the person or their lineage. Also nations and communities can be spiritually unclean even if they look rich and spectacular on the outside.

It is the spiritual uncleanness that is more confusing, not easily detectable and very destructive in the lives of many people and nations.

Spiritual uncleanness is responsible for most generational curses. For instance, a person can be rich, drink alcohol or smoke whatever they choose to smoke, fornicate and take it as part of their social life or a vice in their lives that they have come to accept, not knowing that they engage in such seemingly innocent practices because of generational curses due to unclean spiritual practices of their ancestors. The same can be for a nation.

Outward cleanness, riches or power can be blinding to the spiritual makeup of a person or nation. Generational curses because of spiritual uncleanness can be manifested in the physical realms through such things as unruly or rowdy behavior in a person, family or nation, poverty, excessive murder including abortions or abuse rates, woke ideologies and practices or in spiritual realm in dreams and visions. I believe God allows the manifestations of uncleanness out of his abundant mercy, exposing sin so people can repent and be cleansed. If a person thinks that they are clean, they will never think of seeking repentance.

Spiritual uncleanness can only be resolved spiritually through prayer to the true living God of Abraham, Isaac and Jacob in the name of Jesus Christ and the sacrificial blood Jesus Christ offered at the cross of Calvary for the remission of sin and redemption. Spiritual uncleanness can cause Satan to oppose people.

In the book of Zechariah 3:1-4NKJV, in one of Zechariah's visions, he says the LORD showed him Joshua the high priest standing before the Angel of the LORD, and Satan standing at the right hand to oppose him. And the LORD said to Satan, "The LORD rebuke you, Satan! The LORD who has chosen Jerusalem rebuke you! Is this not a brand plucked from the fire"? The NIV version says, "Is not this man a burning stick snatched from the fire"? Now Joshua was clothed with filthy garments and was standing before the Angel. And He answered and spoke to those who stood before Him, saying "Take away the filthy garments from him." And to him he said "See, I have removed your iniquity from you, and I will clothe you with rich robes. KJV says, "And

I will clothe thee with change of raiment." NIV says, "See, I have taken away your sin, and I will put fine garments on you."

Joshua's physical, visible clothes and appearance was clean. However, his spiritual clothes that were unseen with the naked eye were filthy. Satan was capitalizing on that. A human being has physical garments and spiritual garments. Joshua was an upstanding, holy man who took over from Moses to lead the children of Israel into the Promised Land. However, his spiritual clothes had iniquity that Satan wanted to use to oppose him. The sin found in Joshua could have been from his family line or from his nation. It is only God who appeared in the flesh as the Lord Jesus Christ who can cleanse us from our sins and the iniquities of our predecessors, and change our spiritual clothes and appearance. The appearance of uncleanness in the person's spiritual clothing and makeup because of sin whether of their own or family, is an ammunition for Satan to challenge and afflict people.

Uncleanness refers to the multitude of sins and iniquities of all kinds in one's life or in the life of their ancestors and parents that have never been cleansed by the blood of Jesus Christ. Once the person is cleansed by the blood of Jesus Christ, they are declared clean. A new garment is put on them. In the book of Acts10:14-15, when the Lord spoke to Peter in a vision when he was hungry and saw animal of diverse kinds and was told to take and eat, Peter said to the Lord "Not so Lord! For I have never eaten anything unholy and unclean." And the voice spoke to him a second time "What God has cleansed; you must not call common."

Peter's vision was about sending him to Cornelius, the Gentile and all in his household, to go and proclaim the good news of Jesus Christ for their cleansing and salvation. Once the Lord cleanses us, we are clean.

This cleansing covers and protects any and everything pertaining to born-again Christians. Also, those that are in Christ can plead the blood of Jesus Christ on any and everything to make them clean. This includes food and many items.

The cleansing blood of Jesus Christ is a spiritual weapon against all things' darkness in the physical and spiritual life. The book of Revelation12:11 (NKJV) says, "And they overcame him by the blood of the Lamb and by the word of their testimony, and they did not love their lives to the death.

The Word of God and the Holy Spirit also have cleansing powers. They are also weapons a born-again Christian can use to destroy every spiritual and physical uncleanness. Jesus Christ said in John 6:63 "It is the Spirit who gives life; the flesh profits nothing. The words I speak to you are spirit, and they are life." Again, in Jeremiah 23:29 God says, "Is not my word like a fire? says the LORD, And like a hammer that breaks the rock in pieces?"

Revelation 19:10 says, "Worship God! For the testimony of Jesus Christ is the spirit of prophecy." This is significant because Jesus Christ is the Word of God, through whom all things where made and by whom all things were made and for whom all things were made. It is by hearing the Word of God, that a person obtains the faith to believe and confess that Jesus Christ is their Lord and believe the cleansing power of the blood of Jesus Christ. The Word of God also helps people to come to understand that Jesus Christ is God who came in the flesh to redeem humanity from death and destruction. As people believe, they get cleansed spiritually. Reading the word of God regularly helps born-again Christian maintain their spiritual and physical cleanness. The Word of God, Jesus Christ is living and can never die. In Matthew 24:35, Jesus Christ said "Heaven and earth will pass away, but my words will by no means pass away." In Psalm 119:89, it says, "Forever, O LORD, Your word is settled in heaven."

Psalm 107:15 -20 says, "Oh, that men would give thanks to the LORD for His goodness, and for His wonderful works to the children of men! For He has broken the gates of bronze and cut the bars of iron into two. Fools because of their transgression and because of their iniquities, were afflicted. Their souls abhorred all manner of food, and they drew near the gates of death. Then they cried out to the LORD in their trouble, and He saved them out of their distress. He sent His word, and healed them, and delivered them from their destruction." The word of God that was sent into the earth to heal and deliver people from the destruction of the enemy, Satan, is Jesus Christ, who cleanses us by his blood.

Jesus Christ is the weapon God gave to born-again Christians to fight in the spirit and in the physical. He is the word, the weapon of warfare that is mighty to the pulling down of strongholds. In 2 Corinthians 10: 4-6, it says, "For the weapons of our warfare are not carnal but mighty in God for pulling down strongholds, casting down arguments and every high thing that exalts itself against the knowledge of God, bringing every thought into captivity to the obedience of Christ and being ready to punish all disobedience when your obedience is full."

The obedience of human beings is only made full in Christ. Disobedience is all manner of uncleanness that the enemy uses to go on a rampage to destroy people. The good thing is that the Holy Spirit, who convicts men of sin, helps people to get saved and maintain their cleanness. When the enemy comes in like a flood with uncleanness of any kind to attack born-again Christians, the Holy Spirit raises up a standard against him. In Isaiah 59:19, it says, "When the enemy comes in like a flood, The Spirit of the LORD will lift up a standard against him."

It is through the weapons listed above that believers in Christ are made wholly clean and holy. The spirit of uncleanness cannot stand when the weapons God gave his children are unleashed effectively and intentionally.

Lewdness: This is a cousin of fornication and adultery in the physical and in spiritual realms. Biblehub.com, describes lewdness as immoral and indecent behavior, particularly of a sexual nature. Immoral sexual behavior is a sin against oneself; it harms the person's precious gift, their body.

Our bodies are not our own; they belong to God. In 1 Corinthians 6:15-20, it says, "Do you not know that your bodies are the members of Christ? Shall I then take the members of Christ, and make them the

164

members of an harlot (prostitute)? Certainly not. Or do you not know that he who is joined to an harlot (prostitute) is one body with her?" For "the two," He says, "shall become one flesh." But he who is joined to the Lord is one spirit with Him. Flee sexual immorality. Every sin a man does is outside the body, but he who commits sexual immorality sins against his own body. Or do you not know that your body is the temple of the Holy Spirit who is in you, whom you have from God, and you are not your own? For you were bought at a price; therefore, glorify God in your body and in your spirit, which are God's." This scripture applies only to born-again Christians.

The Bible says the earth is the Lord's and the firmament thereof and everything in it. It means even for non-Christians, their bodies are the Lord's as he has created all people. The human spirit, which keeps people alive, belongs to God and lives in every person's body because it is God who breathes his spirit in every human for each one to have life. Without God's breath of life, no one can live. However, those who are not born-again, their spirit is not made subject to the Holy Spirit and generally refuses to submit to God. Their bodies are not the temple of the Holy Spirit. Their spirits can be manipulated to serving other spirits.

At birth, everyone is separated from God as they are not joined with Christ. To be joined with Christ, it is important that a person be born again, not by flesh (water) and blood, but by the Spirit of the living God. In 1 John 5:7-8 (NKJV), it says there are three (3) witnesses on earth and in heaven. The three witnesses on earth are the Spirit, the water and the blood, and these three agree as one. It takes the three witnesses on earth to agree with each other for a person to be conceived and born. Without the Spirit of the living God, water and blood cannot give birth.

In heaven, the three witnesses are the Father, the Word (Jesus Christ) and the Holy Spirit, and these three are one. Because they are one, they are always in agreement. Rejecting one is to reject all. It takes the three witnesses in heaven to be born-again. A person cannot have God and reject Jesus Christ or the Holy Spirit. It is impossible because the three are one. The work of salvation of the human soul takes God the Father, who sent his one and only begotten Son, Jesus Christ, who is God in the flesh and the Word that created all things to redeem the humanity and is revealed by the Holy Spirit who convicts men of sin and give realization that they need the Savior, Jesus Christ to become the children of God and enter heaven.

Those who refuse to believe and surrender their bodies to God become the masters of their own bodies and can be possessed by the devil, who, in return, controls and owns them. So, when a born again commits the sin of sexual immorality, they are sinning not only against their own self, but against God, Jesus Christ and the Holy Spirit who dwells in them. This is the reason the Bible says flee away from the sin of sexual immorality. Don't contemplate, just flee at first sight.

Romans 11:36 (NLT) says, "For everything comes from him, and exists by his power and is intended for his glory. All glory to him forever. And it continues in 12:1 (NKJV) saying "I beseech you therefore, brethren, by the mercies of God, that you present your bodies as a living sacrifice, holy and acceptable to God, which is your reasonable service."

The enemy's most concerted efforts are to defile the human body with all sorts of sexual immorality, perversions, imaginations and rhetoric. The notion or philosophy that teaches people, especially young women, to say my body, my choice is woke and not of God. It is these kinds of ideologies that make sexual immorality and related sins acceptable to the human soul. Anything that is not of God is of the devil, meant to kill, steal and destroy as well as to separate people from God.

Idolatry: Idolatry, which is spiritual adultery, is an ancient spiritual practice and equivalent to lewdness and whoredom. It is a sin committed against God and brings a lot of curses to families and nations that practice it. It is just like committing adultery against God as it involves worship of other things, deities and graven images as God, the only creator of all things.

With the fall of Adam and Eve, humans became separated from the true God who created them in his image and likeness. Humans have the spirit of God in them and therefore always look for an object of worship that they can revere as superior to themselves. Worship is a language of the spirit. There is a belief that even Satan looks for worship from human beings, hence he has given them diverse religions and spiritual practices that do not worship God Almighty, who came in the flesh on earth to redeem humanity.

Some people even mix church and other things to worship, as the enemy fights for humanity to worship him. In Matthew 4:8-9 (NKJV), Satan said to Jesus Christ, the creator of everything including Satan himself, when he was fasting and hungry, being tempted by the devil, the devil took Him up on an exceedingly high mountain, and showed Him all the kingdoms of the world and their glory, and said "All these things I will give you, if you will fall down and worship me."

He said to Jesus, "If you were to worship me, I will give you all the treasures of the world." This is the devil's strategy to this day, taking humans to high mountains and promising them glory, power, control, fame and wealth. The high mountain the devil takes people to and promises them the world is not a physical mountain. It is a spiritual mountain. There is no mountain on earth from which people can see the whole world at once. Many people have fallen for this temptation and trick of the devil at the high mountain, as people love material and spiritual power, success and control.

Practices like witchcraft, idol worship, yoga and unbiblical meditations of all sorts are about power, control and manipulation. It goes without saying that Satan is desperate for worship, that he promises people and nations material beyond their imagination, only if they can bow and worship him. The worship of Satan comes in many ways. For some is with lifestyle, others with economy, others with false deities and religions, others with false Christianity, others with false spiritual promises and rewards like false heaven where they will be rewarded with many virgins when they die in suicide bombing or for killing people, especially believers in Christ, in the name of a foreign god, others is with material success, fame and prosperity that cannot be sustained for generations. There are many ways to worshipping the devil.

However, there is only one way to worship the true God and enter heaven. The only true worship of God is in the Spirit (Holy Spirit) and in truth (The Word of God, Jesus Christ, who is the only way, the only truth and the only life). The only way to enter heaven is through Jesus Christ and His blood and by His Spirit, the Holy Spirit, who has redeemed sinners and translated those who believe from darkness to light, from hell to heaven, from death to eternal life.

Worship must be the ultimate recognition in the spirit world; otherwise, Satan would not seek it by deceiving and causing people to stumble just so they can worship him. It is not only in the promises of wealth that he gets people to worship him, but also in the empty promises of luxury, popularity, power, and control. All these are empty promises and do not last because in the end, man will die and leave it all behind. Dying without Jesus Christ is the most painful thing. No one's wealth will buy them a ticket to heaven, even if they were to give it all away to the poor. It is not by good deeds that people enter heaven. People must believe and confess that Jesus Christ came in the flesh and is their Lord and Savior.

Wealth, fame, power, control, popularity, saints, false gods and all the promises of Satan easily become items of worship for those who possess them, their fans and followers. The devil is not able to bless, as blessings are a gift from God. Because Satan gives with one hand and collects with another, his offerings are with sorrow. Sometimes, people lose whatever they had gained by worshipping their idols even when they are still alive. Imagine a politician or celebrity who chooses to engage in occult, signing a deal with the devil to win elections for a 4-year term and thereafter lose the next elections and find themselves with nothing really. Some go deeper into darkness and commit corruption and take bribes, kickbacks and all sorts of unscrupulous practices to stay in positions of power, renewing their evil covenants with the devil to avoid the embarrassment of living an ordinary life after a high life of power. This power can be intellectual, political, spiritual, economic, material and social and very addictive.

Also, the illusion of power and control can be strong. It is what makes people join many ungodly clubs, secret societies and the like. Also, a person can have all the money in the world and fame that comes with it and never live long on earth to enjoy it. Somewhere, the enemy gets them with sickness, torments beyond imagination or disgrace. Proverbs 13:22 says, "A good man leaves an inheritance to his children's children, but the sinner's wealth is laid up for the righteous."

Some rich and famous people end up in jail, hopeless and regretting their pact with the devil. Somewhere, the devil will afflict pain and attack the people who choose him because he hates all humanity. When such troubles come, those without Jesus Christ become hopeless, especially when they find out that money cannot buy health or peace in their lives. It is an evil thing to reject the gospel of Jesus Christ and salvation through Christ and choose the path of the prince of the powers of the air, the devil.

Christians do encounter challenges and difficulties. The difference is Jesus Christ and the Holy Spirit operating in their lives. Their worship of God gives them hope and victory, even if they die in their afflictions. They do not lose hope even unto death. Their hope is not in their own power, abilities, material solutions or spiritual solutions outside the creator of the world, who knows all things, is ever present and all-powerful. Whether a Christian dies from sickness, they die with hope because their death means the beginning of their eternal life with Christ. 2 Corinthians 5:8 (NKJV) says to be absent from the body is to be present with the Lord. For born-again Christians, there is hope in life and in death. When trouble comes and the person has no Jesus Christ and the Holy Spirit in them and by their side, it becomes a pitiful and hopeless case. God is the hope of those who worship him in spirit and in truth and have put their complete trust and faith in him. Jesus Christ came to give us hope in a hopeless world.

Idolatry is a sin that defiles people spiritually. Worshipping other gods or other things such as graven images, wealth, power, control, or people is idolatry and a defilement to the person's spirit and soul. The time God gives to people on earth is precious and should not be wasted in idolatry. When people are born, no one knows how much time each will have here on earth.

Every day a person is on earth is the day of salvation that is only found in Jesus Christ. This is very urgent.

The ultimate purpose of humanity is to worship God through the name of Jesus Christ and by His Spirit and through His blood. The blood of Jesus Christ has reconciled humanity with God, those who choose to believe and surrender. God came in the flesh in the world to destroy the works of the devil and was embodied in Jesus Christ. God, through the cross of Calvary, has given humanity a holy altar established by a new covenant in the blood of Jesus. Idolatry goes hand in hand with evil altars and evil covenants and can only be destroyed in a person's life and in nations by the blood of Jesus Christ.

Sorcery: Now this is a very interesting aspect of the works of the flesh. Sorcery is an evil spirit, and those who practice sorcery are possessed by the spirit of sorcery. It is a very dangerous spiritual practice. Sorcery is very evil. Sorcerers are humans who have availed themselves to be used by the enemy. They are very dangerous weapons of the enemy. Sorcery is equated with magic and closely related to witchcraft. It is the practice of bewitching people through various practices and using spiritual laws and natural elements to attack people, places, environments, lives, destinies and many other things that are valuable to people or nations. It is the ultimate desperation for control. It involves manipulating people, places, environments, and conditions through spiritual means for gain or harm.

According to Biblehub.com, sorcery is defined as "the practice of using supernatural powers or magic, often through the assistance of evil spirits, to influence events or manipulate people. The term is frequently associated with witchcraft, divination and the occult." The Bible condemns sorcery at all levels. The fact that the Bible speaks about sorcery means it exists. Spiritual things are not seen with a human eye. The practices and results of sorcery can be seen with the naked eye, but the processes that cause the results are unseen. In Hebrews 11:3 (NKJV) it says, "By faith we understand that the worlds were framed by the word of God, so that the things which are seen were not made of things which are visible." This is a spiritual principle that the enemy has taught his evil agents, the sorcerers to do evil.

The magicians of Pharaoh, Jannes and Jambres, who contended with Moses, resisting the departure of the children of Israel from Egypt, the land of their slavery, were sorcerers. Exodus 7:11-12. That's what sorcerers do, they resist the plan of God and good things in the lives of people and want to enslave people through evil powers. The wise men of Nebuchadnezzar were sorcerers. Mediums who practice necromancy, the speaking with the dead, calling the dead, worshipping the dead and getting messages from the dead, are sorcerers. The witch or medium Saul went to so he could get a word from Samuel, who was dead, was a sorcerer. The lady in the book of Acts who helped her masters to make money was a sorcerer.

Before the gospel of Jesus Christ came into the world, many people and nations relied on those with evil powers who practiced sorcery. In Acts 8:5-11 (NKJV), it says, "Then Phillip went down to the city of Samaria and preached Christ to them. And the multitudes with one accord heeded the things spoken by Phillip, hearing and seeing the miracles which he did. For unclean spirits, crying with a loud voice, came out of many who were possessed, and many who were paralyzed, and the lame were healed. And there was great joy in that city. But there was a certain man, called Simon, who previously practiced sorcery in the city and astonished the people of Samaria, claiming that he was someone great; to whom they all gave heed, from the least to the greatest, saying, "This man is the great power of God." And they heeded him because he had astonished them with his sorcery for a long time." One wonders how many ancient and recent kingdoms ruled people using sorcery and how many organizations, governments and leaders in all strata of life today rule using sorcery.

When people don't have the gospel of Jesus Christ, they call any power and magic, the power of God. This is how Satan keeps many in darkness. They go to the shrines of darkness, where they see power generated with evil spirits, and they get convinced that they are in the right place. This is why the world is filled with religions, spiritual practices and beliefs away from the gospel. The existence of false religions keeps sorcery active, alive and pervasive on the earth. Not to mention occult practices and secret societies. The world is ruled by and filled with sorcery for the most part.

Where there is no Christ, there is sorcery. The power, miracles and wonders seen are from the devil, evil spirits disguised as light and true power. Many are deceived, and it has been for generations.

Many kings of the ancient world, even the Roman Empire, used the services of sorcerers to rule and exert power and control. The Roman Empire practiced paganism, which is the worship of evil spirits and sorcery. Even the wealthy people in the early Bible days in Greece and other places practiced paganism. The Apostles of Jesus Christ encountered a lot of sorcery when they were spreading the gospel throughout the world. When Paul and Silas travelled to Philippi, which is in Greece and was a Roman colony, they encountered a sorcerer. It says in the book of Acts 16:16-21 (NKJV), "Now it happened, as we went to prayer, that a certain slave girl possessed with a spirit of divination met us, who brought her masters much profit by fortune-telling. This girl followed Paul and us, and cried out, saying, "These men are the servants of the Most High God, who proclaim to us the way of salvation." And this she did for many days. But Paul, greatly annoyed, turned and said to the spirit, "I command you in the name of Jesus Christ to come out of her." And he came out that very hour. But when her masters saw that their hopes of profit (making money) was gone, they seized Paul and Silas and dragged them into the marketplace to the authorities, and they brought them to the magistrates, and said "These men, being Jews, exceedingly trouble our city, and they teach customs which are not lawful for us, being Romans, to receive or observe."

Again in Athens, in Acts 17:22-24 (NKJV), it says, "Then Paul stood in the midst of the Areopagus and said "Men of Athens, I perceive that in all things you are very religious; for as I was passing through and considering the objects of your worship, I even found an altar with this inscription, 'TO THE UNKOWN GOD'. Therefore, the One whom you worship without knowing, Him I proclaim to you. God, who made the world and everything in it, since he is Lord of heaven and earth, does not dwell in temples made with hands. Nor is he worshipped with men's hands, as though he needed anything, since he gives to all life, breath, and all things."

It goes without saying that some of the religious and spiritual practices people engage in and have come to revere and honor are sorcery. Any religious and spiritual practice without Jesus Christ as the focal point and fails to acknowledge Jesus Christ as the Son of God who came in the flesh can be classified as sorcery. It is anti-Christ and draws spiritual power from strange spirits.

I believe the anti-Christ spirit is also the spirit of sorcery because a false prophet manipulates and deceives people, sometimes even coerces them to follow him. Sorcery involves the manipulation and control of people's minds, hearts, souls, spirits, life and possessions. The Bible says we are to test every spirit. In 1 John 4:1 (NKJV) it says, "Beloved, do not believe every spirit, but test the spirits, whether they are of God, because many false prophets have gone out into the world." It continues in 1 John 4:3 saying "and every spirit that does not confess that Jesus Christ has come in the flesh is not of God. And this is the spirit of the anti-Christ, which you have heard was coming, and is now already in the world."

Not everything and everyone that looks holy on the outside is holy. Sorcery can be difficult to detect. The Bible says in 2 Corinthians 11:14 that "even Satan disguises himself as an angel of light." The Spirit of the living God, the Holy Spirit, who dwells in born-again Christians, helps and enables Christians to identify the operation of sorcery even in seemingly innocent environments and people.

Since spirits do not die, the spirit of sorcery has been passed on in this world from generation to generation to this day. It operates in the people and places that refuse to repent and take Jesus Christ as their Lord and Savior. The gospel of Jesus Christ, belief and faith in Him alone, is the only powerful antidote to sorcery.

Enmities/Hatred: Hatred is a spirit and a very evil one. It is a deep-rooted negative emotion towards anything or anyone. It is the opposite of love. Love is a spirit, and God is Love. God is Spirit. If Love is spirit and God is love, it means hatred is also a spirit and the devil is hatred. Love and hatred are very strong spirits and emotions. As people, we need to guard our hearts to ensure that we love more than we hate. Both hate and love can make people do honorable or dishonorable things against others. Love can make a person forgive someone who has done painful, hurtful things against them. Hate can make a person want to take revenge and destroy the person who has done painful, hurtful things against them.

People can hate, and it is important that the things people hate are sin and sinful acts. No one can truly love God and love sin and sinful acts. Those who love God, hate sin.

I recall one dream, more like a vision, I had, and the Lord Jesus Christ revealed the degree of hatred Satan possesses. The hate was so deep and thick. His hatred was so alive that you could touch it. It was unbelievable. I have never seen or experienced such deep hatred as I did in that vision. When they say Satan hates humanity, it is true. His hatred compares to nothing I have ever seen or heard about on earth. We have heard in the news and seen on TV heinous things done to others by seriously evil people. I believe the people who go out to kill, steal and destroy, carry out suicide bombings and terror attacks, are possessed by the spirit of hatred. No one can hate so deeply without being possessed by Satan himself. Satan can possess nations, religions, people, institutions, organizations, families, and racial groups which practice hatred to others in their own way. The antisemitic actions and rhetoric, as well as persecutions of Christians in the world stem from deep hatred Satan has for the Jews and the Christians. Hatred is a spiritual thing, just as love is a spiritual thing. The sad thing is that the devil has managed to convince the lost people and nations that the Bible preaches hate speech when it teaches love. It is a loving thing to expose sin and help people to repent.

The one thing that distinguishes Christianity and practicing Christians from other religions, faiths and people is the Love of Jesus Christ in them. God is Love, and God and Jesus Christ are one.

Jesus Christ is God who came in the flesh. In Matthew 5:43-48 (NKJV), Jesus Christ said, "You have heard that it was said, 'You shall love your neighbor and hate your enemy'. But I say to you, love your enemies, bless those who curse you, do good to those who hate you, and pray for those who spitefully use you and persecute you, that you may be sons of your Father in heaven; for He makes His sun rise on the evil and on the good, and sends rain on the just and on the unjust. For if you love those who love you, what reward have you? Do not even the tax collectors do the same? And if you greet your brethren only, what do you do more than others? Do not even the tax collectors do so? Therefore, you shall be perfect, just as your Father in heaven is perfect."

The Bible equates hatred with murder. 1 John 3:15 says, "Whoever hates his brother is a murderer, and you know that no murderer has eternal life abiding in him." Jesus Christ also said that the devil is a murderer. In John 8:44 (NIV), when the Pharisees wanted to capture Jesus Christ to kill him, Jesus Christ said to them, "You belong to your father, the devil, and you want to carry out your father's desires. He was a murderer from the beginning, not holding to the truth, for there is no truth in him. When he lies, he speaks his native language, for he was a liar and the father of lies."

Contention/Strife: Strife and contention are spirits that cause divisions among people. These spirits must be resisted at all costs. Acts of contention and strife are completely disapproved, especially among Christians. They are destructive acts and words that affect human relations and emotions negatively. The spirits of strife and contention are closely connected to the spirits of anger, envy and jealousy. On Biblehub.com, contention and strife are described as conflict, discord, and disputes among individuals and groups, and are indicative of a breakdown in relationships and are generally portrayed as negative attributes that disrupt peace and unity.

It is important to resolve strife and contention quickly. Jesus Christ gave numerous antidotes for strife and contention. Forgiveness and peace help curb strife and contention. In the Lord's Prayer, we are reminded to forgive others so our sins can be forgiven. This implies that if you do not forgive others, God will not forgive you, even if you ask for forgiveness. In Matthew 6:14-15 (NKJV), Jesus said, "For if you forgive men their trespass, your heavenly Father will also forgive you. But if you do not forgive men their trespass, neither will your Father forgive your trespasses." Where there is unforgiveness, strife and contentions persist.

Forgiveness is a big deal. It can be the most difficult thing to do, especially when the person is hurt and shattered. When it is difficult to forgive, a person can pray for God to give them a heart to forgive.

It takes a lot of spiritual and emotional maturity to forgive. We are encouraged to forgive quickly. On the cross of Calvary, while being crucified, when the pain was intense and people were merciless toward him, Jesus Christ said something very profound and enlightening about forgiveness. In Luke 23:34 (NKJV), Jesus Christ said, "Father, forgive them, for they do not know what they do." Jesus Christ asked God to forgive those who crucified him, and those people represented all of humanity. The evidence of that forgiveness was manifested when the Lord asked Peter to go to the house of the Gentile Cornelius, who is noted to have been the first gentile person to be baptized with all in his household. This communicates that salvation in Jesus Christ is not limited to its Jewish origin; it is for all who seek the God of heaven and earth earnestly, whether Gentile or Jew. For humanity to receive salvation is because God has forgiven the gruesome actions that the Jews and the Gentiles inflicted on Jesus Christ. It was very important for the sin to be forgiven so that Satan does not interfere and disturb the will of God to save humanity.

Unforgiveness is a sin, hence the Lord ask us to forgive others and ask that we be forgiven by God and those we trespass against. It is important to bear in mind that the spiritual and emotional maturity necessary to forgive has nothing to do with age. It is the Holy Spirit who helps Christians to have the spiritual and emotional maturity to forgive.

Unforgiveness is food for the enemy. It is one of the spiritual gates and doors the enemy uses to accuse people before God and to afflict lives. Unforgiveness goes hand in hand with offense. Unchecked strife and contention can be the breeding ground of offense and unforgiveness, and this can break families, nations, communities and companies. Proverbs 15:18 (NKJV) says, "A wrathful man stirs up strife, but he who is slow to anger allays/calms contention." If not dealt with, unforgiveness can become a generational curse in families, racial groups, religious groups and nations.

Another antidote for strife and contention that Jesus Christ taught is peace-loving and peace-making. I believe in his Sermon on the Mount, called The Beatitudes, Jesus Christ also addresses the issue of strife and contention. Matthew 5:9 says, "Blessed are the peacemakers, for they shall be called the sons of God."

Where there is peace, there is no strife. The Bible gives strategies to resolve strife and contention. In Proverbs 17:14 (NKJV), it says, "The beginning of strife is like releasing water, therefore stop contention before a quarrel starts." Some Bible versions say it is like releasing a flood. It is difficult to control a flood. The best is to never let it out or cause it. Never give place to strife. It is to be avoided.

Peace, humility, forgiveness and kindness are great antidotes against strife and contention. Jesus Christ urges Christians to make peace quickly with their adversaries.

In Matthew 5:25-26 (NKJV), Jesus says, "Agree with your adversary quickly, while you are on the way with him, lest your adversary deliver you to the judge, the judge hand you over to the officer, and you be thrown into prison. Assuredly, I say to you, you will by no means get out of there till you have paid the last penny." It takes humility to do what Jesus Christ say we must do in cases of opposition. Pride stops people from settling disputes quickly until destruction strikes. In Proverbs 28:25, it says, "He who is of a proud heart, stirs up strife, but he who trusts in the Lord will be prospered."

Romans 12:14-21 (NKJV) says, "Bless those who persecute you, bless and do not curse. Rejoice with those who rejoice, and weep with those who weep. Be of the same mind toward one another. Do not set your mind on high things (pride/do not be proud) but associate with the humble. Do not be wise in your own opinion. Repay no one evil for evil. Have regard for good things in the sight of all men. If it is possible, as much as depends on you, live peaceably with all men. Beloved, do not avenge yourselves, but rather give place to wrath, for it is written, "Vengeance is Mine, I will repay," says the Lord. Therefore, "If your enemy is hungry, feed him, if he is thirsty, give him a drink; for in so doing you will heap coals of fire on his head." Do not be overcome by evil, but overcome evil with good."

It takes a humble heart to bless people who want to destroy you. When a Christian does not respond to persecution, contention and hatred, it does not mean they are stupid and naive. They are wise because they know that engaging a person who values strife and contention is unwise, as God has promised to deal with those people on their behalf. What a Christian needs to do is to give the issue and the person to God for vengeance and continue to be peaceful, kind, humble and bless those people. This is a spiritual response and the power that cannot be underestimated.

Pride, arrogance, jealousy, hatred, envy, hurt and such things are typical sources of vengeance against those who are believed to have caused strife and contention. Some people do not respond directly in the physical but respond in the spirit. A spiritual response is the most powerful and can be the most destructive and difficult to deal with, and resolve. Where people are driven by evil desires to cause harm using evil powers, their acts can be the most destructive. When God is the one avenging, it is for correction and vindication. God is fair and just. This is the reason the Bible says do not repay evil for evil and not provoke or cause others to do evil.

Give it to God, because vengeance belongs to him. This is to protect Christians from spiritual retaliation. Maintaining a life of peace and forgiving quickly helps to keep strife and contention away from one's life.

Jealousies: This is another dangerous, demonic spirit. Jealousy is evil and a poison to the human soul, mind and heart. It is a relative of anger and bitterness. In the context of the Bible, jealousy is expressed as a positive or a negative. When it comes to the acts of the flesh, jealousy is a negative that produces sinful outcomes. It takes jealousy to be a witch, be competitive, hate good things when they happen to others, and covet what others have. In James 3:14-16, it says, "But if you have bitter jealousy and selfish ambition in your hearts, do not boast and be false to the truth. This is not the wisdom that comes down from above, but is earthly, unspiritual, and demonic. For where jealousy and selfish ambition exist, there will be disorder and every vile thing."

Proverbs 27:4 says, "Wrath is cruel, anger is overwhelming, but who can stand before jealousy?" The thing with jealousy is that it can be harbored inside, hidden too deep inside the heart of a person who seems kind, polite and helpful on the outside but cruel and evil on the inside. Jealousy can cause a person or people to secretly connive evil against others.

1 Corinthians 3:3 (ESV) says, "For you are still of the flesh. For while there is jealousy and strife among you, are you not of the flesh and behaving only in a human way?"

Jealousy is driven by things we see and hear in the world that pollute the heart, the mind and the soul, the human faculties we do not see with our naked eye. It is so destructive in that it destroys both the perpetrator and their targets. Once jealousy is conceived in the heart, it gives birth to evil outcomes.

When a Christian is not transformed by the Spirit of the living God in their hearts, the spirit of jealousy can easily enter. It is critical that a Christian hunger and cry for the baptism of the Holy Spirit to help them not to fall into the traps of the enemy in the flesh. In Exodus 20:17, God says, "You shall not covet your neighbor's house; you shall not covet your neighbor's wife, or his male servant, or his female servant, or his ox, or his donkey or anything that is your neighbor's." This implies that it is easy for an unguarded heart to fall into the trap of jealousy.

The Bible urges Christians to rejoice with those who rejoice and mourn with those who mourn. This is a great antidote against jealousy.

Outbursts of wrath: This refers to excessive, unrighteous anger that causes sinful acts. Outbursts of wrath are a sin. Wrath is a spirit that drives a lot of killings, murders, and revenge among people and nations. It is closely related to bitterness and offence.

There is righteous anger and unrighteous anger. Righteous anger leads to correction and repentance, and unrighteous anger leads to destruction. Christian can get angry against sin and the works of the enemy. The Bible says to be angry but not sin. Ephesians 4:26-27 (NKJV) says, "Be angry, and not sin. Do not let the sun go down on your wrath, nor give place to the devil."

Outbursts of wrath can be a door for the devil to come into a person's life. Unrighteous anger seeks to destroy and avenge. The Bible says vengeance is the Lord's. In Romans 12:19 (NKJV), it says, "Beloved, do not avenge yourselves, but rather give place to wrath; for it is written

"Vengeance Is Mine, I Will Repay," Says The Lord."

Righteous anger is indignation for sin and the works of the enemy. It abhors sin and evil works. Righteous anger can cause people to act against the evil works of the enemy, seek help such as deliverance, come to Jesus Christ for salvation, and be driven to take acts of kindness. Righteous anger can result in acts that instill godliness, holiness, honor, hope, respect and the fear of God.

Jesus Christ had righteous anger when he entered the temple and found people conducting their businesses in the House of God without the fear of God. The temple was a place where people were to come and worship and not engage in commercial activities. He overturned the tables to correct the sinners and called people to repentance. Matthew 21:12-14 (NKJV) says, "Then Jesus went into the temple of God and drove out all those who bought and sold in the temple and overturned the tables of the money changers and the seats of those who sold doves." And He said to them, "It is written, 'My house shall be called a house of prayers,' but you have made it a den of thieves. Then the blind and the lame came to Him in the temple, and He healed them."

The temple was his house. It broke his heart to see people engage in ungodly practices in his house. Jesus took the act of correcting the sinners who were disrespecting and dishonoring the house of God by turning it into a marketplace, taking advantage of the people who came to do sacrifices at the temple. Those buying were equally guilty, as they caused ungodly businesses to thrive in the house of God. Today, some churches are not only places of worship and prayer but also places of commerce. They sell many things, including coffee, tea, food of all kinds, spiritual items, church or pastor branded merchandise and sermons.

Jesus Christ equated the selling in the church with stealing, saying they have turned the temple into a den of thieves. Those who sell at the church, therefore, qualify as thieves according to the Bible. As we know, in the Bible, it is the thief who comes to steal, kill and destroy. In John 10:10 (NKJV), Jesus Christ said, "The thief does not come except to steal, and to kill and to destroy. I have come that they may have life, and that they may have it more abundantly." When Jesus Christ rebuked the evil works in the temple, he was not angry. After getting the thieves out of the temple, he then performed a loving act of healing to those who were sick in the temple.

When Moses announced to Pharaoh that at midnight God would pass through the land of Egypt and the first-born of human and animals will die, he was burning with righteous anger against Pharaoh's sin of disobedience and stubbornness. In Exodus 11:8 (NLT), He said to Pharaoh, "All the officials of Egypt will run to me and fall to the ground before me 'Please leave,' they will beg, 'hurry and take all your followers with you,' only then will I go." Then, burning with anger, Moses left Pharaoh. This was a righteous anger toward Pharaoh's disobedience to God's instructions.

The Bible warns Christians to be angry but not sin. Excessive anger could be destructive. Pharaoh had excessive unrighteous anger toward the children of Israel when he was asked to let them go out of the land of their slavery in Egypt so they could worship God. He therefore remained stubborn even in the face of nine plagues that ravaged Egypt, and to his demise and the demise of many in Egypt. Excessive anger can harden the heart and breed a stubborn attitude, driven by the spirit of sorcery.

Selfish ambitions: These include actions and deeds that are done for self-glory and not for the glory of God, and seek self-recognition even if they are done as acts of kindness. The Bible says in all things, we should give God the glory. 1 Corinthians 10:31 (ESV) says, "So whether you eat or drink, or whatever you do, do all to the glory of God." Selfish ambitions give glory to self-strength, self-power, abilities and capabilities. It is the spirit of self-centeredness and self-pride. Whatever the person does is for their self-satisfaction and benefit. Pride, including self-pride and seeking the praises of men are the source of selfish ambitions and the nature of the devil.

As children of God, we are empowered by the Holy Spirit. We are here to do the will of God by his power and not our will by our power. We are here to glorify God, as he is the one giving us wisdom, ability, capabilities, and the breath of life for us to achieve success and reach our destinies. He gives us the desires of our hearts. Jesus Christ said in John 15:5 (NKJV) that "I am the vine; you are the branches. He who abides in me, and I in him, bears much fruit; for without me you can do nothing." A born-again Christian who functions without Jesus Christ can easily fall into the trap of selfish ambitions, limited in the world of self and open a door for the enemy in their lives to steal, kill and destroy.

This also applies to prayer. Prayer driven by self-ambition is praying amiss. James 4:3 (NKJV) says, "You ask and do not receive, because you ask amiss, that you may spend it on your pleasures." It is important to pray in line with the will of God. The will of God is the word of God. Prayer needs to align with the word of God. When people rely on prayer and Jesus Christ, they pray and receive answers. They are inclined to glorify God because they know that without God, they could not have achieved what their heart desires. Relying on God's provision takes away the spirit of selfish ambitions.

The Bible says in Revelation 5:12 that power, and riches, and wisdom, and strength, and honor and glory, and blessings belong to God, to Jesus Christ. Knowing that all these come from our Lord and Savior Jesus Christ and not from oneself destroys the spirit of self-pride and selfish ambitions and keeps us humble.

In James 3:16 (NIV), it says, "For where you have envy and selfish ambition, there you find disorder and every evil practice." Selfish ambition is an enemy of humility and goes hand in hand with strife, jealousy, envy and bitterness. Competitions and desire to be on top for self-glory and praise from people can result in selfish ambitions being the driving force for whatever the person wants to achieve. Matthew 5:16 (ESV), says, "In the same way, let your light shine before others, so that they may see your good works and give glory to your Father who is in heaven." Bottom line, all glory belongs to God.

Philippians 2:3-4 (NKJV), says, "Let nothing be done through selfish ambition or conceit, but in lowliness of mind let each esteem others better than himself. Let each of you look out not only for his own interest, but also for the interests of others." The antidote against self-ambitions is thanksgiving and love. Colossians 3:17 (ESV) says, "And whatever you do, in word or deed, do everything in the name of the Lord Jesus, giving thanks to God the Father through him."

In 1 Corinthians 13:1-3 it says, "Though I speak with the tongues of men and of angels, but have not love, I have become sounding brass or clanging cymbal. And though I have the gift of prophecy, and understand all mysteries and all knowledge, and though I have all faith, so that I could remove mountains, but have not love, I am nothing. And though I bestow all my goods to feed the poor, and though I give my body to be burned, but have not love, it profits me nothing." Without love, whatever good the person does, it is done for self-glory, for self-recognition, and for the praises of men, and therefore hypocritical.

Jesus Christ rebuked the Pharisees and the scribes for their hypocrisy and selfish ambitions in Matthew 23:13-33 and Luke 11:39-52. The Pharisees, scribes and lawyers were looking good and holy to everyone on the outside, but on the inside, selfish ambitions and desires ruled and reigned, influencing their attitudes. This is the reason they were jealous and troubled by the presence of Jesus Christ. They perceived him as a threat to their professional and material successes as well as their prestige in society, as many people turned to Jesus Christ for teaching, healing and deliverance.

Dissensions: Dissension is a spirit and constitutes disagreements that result in divisions. The (KJV) dictionary defines dissension as disagreement in opinion, usually a disagreement which is violent, producing warm debates or angry words; contention in words; strife; discord; quarrel; breach of friendship and union.

According to Proverbs 6:16-19 (NKJV), dissention (discord) is one of the seven things that the Lord hates and is abomination to God. It says, "These six things the LORD hates, yes, seven are an abomination (testable) unto him; A proud look, a lying tongue, and hands that shed innocent blood, a heart that devise wicked plans, feet that are swift in running to evil, a false witness who speaks lies, and one who sows discord among brethren (family)." Dissension can be planted among people. The great antidote against dissension is self-control, which is the Fruit of the Holy Spirit. Without self-control, people can easily be carried away by violent emotions and disagreements.

Unity and peaceable living are also antidotes against dissensions. People do not have to agree on everything. However, they must be united in thought, ambition/purpose, and belief to avoid dissensions. In 1 Corinthians 1:10 -13 (NIV), Paul says, "I appeal to you, brothers and sisters, in the name of our Lord Jesus Christ, that all of you agree with one another in what you say and that there be no division among you, but that you be perfectly united in mind and thought/purpose."

As unity goes with peace, in Romans 12:18 (ESV), it says, "If possible, so far as it depends on you, live peaceably with all." This implies that peaceable life is a choice people make, and the opposite is also true. Self-control implies that, as people, we need not respond to everything that challenges us. We should take all our challenges to God. There will be things on earth that will challenge anyone to maintain a peaceful life with everyone. However, in every situation, peace must be the focus. One of Jesus Christ's teachings in the Sermon on the Mount, "the beatitudes" Matthew 5:9 (KJV), he says, "Blessed are the peacemakers, for they shall be called the children of God."

Settling disputes before they blow up is also critical for maintaining peace and avoiding dissensions. In Matthew 5:25-26 (NKJV), Jesus Christ says, "Agree with your adversary quickly, while you are on your way with him (to court), lest your adversary deliver you to the judge, the judge hand you over to the officer, and you be thrown into prison. Assuredly I say to you, you will by no means get out of there till you have paid the last penny." Failure to seek peace with those who disagree with you can escalate things to a point of heavy penalties. Your enemies can choose to exert the maximum pain. It might look weak and naïve to seek peace, but it is a powerful weapon in the spirit realms.

Dissensions can grieve the Holy Spirit. It can affect and hinder the manifestation of the power of God and the move of the Holy Spirit. Sometimes, it takes wisdom from God to resolve dissensions. In 1

Kings 3:16-28 (NKJV), Solomon used the wisdom from God to resolve the discord between the two mothers who were arguing who is the mother of the living child and who is the mother of the dead child. It says in verse 28 that "And all Israel heard of the judgment which the king had rendered; and they feared the king, for they saw that the wisdom of God was in him to administer justice."

This is also demonstrated in Acts 6:1-7 when the disciples increased and constituted various ethnic and diverse groups. It says, "Now in those days, when the number of disciples was multiplying, there arose a complaint against the Hebrews by the Hellenists, because their widows were neglected in daily distribution. Then the twelve summoned the multitude of the disciples and said "It is not desirable that we should leave the word of God and serve tables. Therefore brethren, seek out from among you seven men of good reputation, full of the Holy Spirit and wisdom, whom we may appoint over this business, but we will give ourselves continually to prayer and to the ministry of the word." And the saying pleased the whole multitude. And they chose Stephen, a man full of faith and the Holy Spirit, and Phillip, Prochorus, Nicanor, Timon, Parmenas, and Nicolas, a proselyte from Antioch, whom they set before the apostles, and when they had prayed, they laid hands on them. Then the word of God spread, and the number of the disciples multiplied greatly in Jerusalem, and a great many priests were obedient to the faith." Resolving the conflict peacefully distinguished the apostles and pleased the disciples, who even multiplied as the word of God was preached because the apostles were free from daily chores to spread the word of God.

Heresies/factions: This relates to the denial of the sound doctrine of the word of God. It denies the doctrine that says salvation comes not by anyone else or anything but by Jesus Christ alone, and that Jesus Christ is the only way to the Father, he is the way, the truth and the life. I believe heresies are the expressions of the spirit of the anti-Christ.

Heresies are false doctrines that look like Christian teachings but lead people astray and far away from the true God. 2 Peter 2:1-22 details heretics and the consequences of following heretical teachings that entice weak souls. Heresies are the teachings and spiritual practices of false prophets and teachers. With so many factions of Christianity, heresies abound. Heretics are presumptuous and self-willed. In 2 Peter 2:15, heretical prophets and teachers are equated to Balaam, a prophet in the Old Testament who loved the wages of unrighteousness and was hired by Balak, the king of Moab, one of the ancient kings who hated Israel, to curse the children of Israel for monetary gain and gifts. False prophets and teachers who are driven by money and do what they do for personal gain tend to be heretical. Heresies are destructive in nature and can fool many.

In 2 Peter 2:1-3, it says, "But there were also false prophets among the people, even as there will be false teachers among you, who will secretly bring in destructive heresies, even denying the Lord who bought them, and bring on themselves swift destruction. And many will follow their destructive ways, because of whom the way of truth will be blasphemed. By covetousness they will exploit you with deceptive words, for a long time their judgment has not been idle, and their destruction does not slumber." I believe destruction in this passage refers to the teachings and church practices that subtly lead people in the wrong spiritual path away from the true God.

Those who teach falsehood exploit their followers for material gain.

Heresies are a sign of the last days. It says in 2 Timothy 4:3-4 (NKJV) that "For the time will come when they will not endure sound doctrine, but according to their own desires, because they have itching ears, they will heap up for themselves teachers; and they will turn their ears away from the truth and be tuned aside to fables." The doctrine that is comfortable and fails to convict people of sin is very dangerous. A feel-good gospel has become accepted, especially as some teachers of the word want to fit in and move with the times, embracing earthly ideologies such as diversity and inclusion. They tend to teach what is acceptable to the majority and to keep the numbers for personal financial gains. Heresies can lead people to hell.

Jesus Christ says in Matthew 7:13-14 (NJKV and KJV), "Enter by the narrow gate, for wide is the gate, and broad is the way that leads to destruction, and there are many who go in by it, because strait is the gate and narrow is the way, which leadeth unto life, and few there be that find it."

Any church or preacher that tells people there are many ways to God, is flexible with the gospel, denies Jesus Christ as the only Savior and Lord, but replaces him with themselves or make him equal to other objects of worship, such as Mary or dead saints or ideologies that contradict the truth of the gospel of Jesus Christ, is a heretic. 2 Peter 2 clarifies the issue of heresies and false teachers and speaks strongly against such. Without reading the Bible for oneself with the help of the Holy Spirit, who reveals God's word, it is easy to fall into the hands of the heretics and believe in heresy.

Envy: Envy is an evil spirit. It is closely related to jealousy. It is a strong desire to be in someone's position or have what they have. To avoid envy, it is important to have the spirit of self-control. The Bible urges people in Romans 12:15 (NKJV) to "rejoice with those who rejoice, and weep with those who weep." This can help to curb the spirit of envy as you allow people's joy to be your joy and their pain to be your pain and not regard yourself higher.

The spirit of envy is very wicked. Those afflicted with the spirit of envy could even envy sin and sinful people. Proverbs 23:14 says, "Do not let your heart envy sinners, but always be zealous for the fear of the LORD."

God is Love. Where there is love, there is no room for envy. Romans 12:9-10 (NIV) says, "Love must be sincere. Hate what is evil; cling to what is good. Be devoted to one another in love. Honor one another above yourselves." Having love in the heart and operating from a position of love destroys envy. Without the Holy Spirit, love has no room in a person's heart.

Honoring others also helps to eliminate the spirit of envy. 1 Corinthians 13:4 says, "Love is patient, love is kind. It does not envy, it does not boast, it is not proud." Love, kindness and meekness are the Fruit of the Holy Spirit which help to keep envy at bay. Also, the fear of God and honoring others remove the spirit of envy from the heart.

A child of God has no need to envy anyone or anything. God is the giver of good things to his righteous people who walk with uprightness of heart and are humble to ask. Jesus Christ says in Matthew 7:11 (NKJV), "If you then, being evil, know how to give good gifts to your children, how much more will your Father who is in heaven give good things to those who ask Him."

In the Bible, we learn that Satan fell from grace because of his envy and jealousy toward God. In Isaiah 14:12-14 (ESV), it says, "How you are fallen from heaven, O Day Star, son of dawn! How are you cut down to the ground, you who laid the nations low! You said in your heart 'I will ascend to heaven; above the stars of God, I will set my throne on high; I will sit on the mount of assembly in the far reaches of the north; I will ascend above the heights of the clouds; I will make myself like the Most-High." We also know that this envy did not get him anywhere. He was thrown out of heaven. Jesus Christ said in Luke 10:18 (NKJV), "I saw Satan fall like lightning from heaven."

The envy of Satan towards God causes Satan to disguise himself as the angel of light to fool people into thinking they are worshipping and serving God while they follow in the ways of the devil. The spirit of envy is also behind the spirit of false worship, religion, greed, atheism, evolution and all related ideologies. In 2 Corinthians 11:14 (ESV), it says, "And no wonder, for even Satan disguises himself as an angel of light. In Corinthians 4:4 (ESV), it says, "In their case, the god of this world has blinded the minds of the unbelievers, to keep them from seeing the light of the gospel of the glory of Christ, who is the image of God."

Envy, just like jealousy, outbursts of wrath and competition, can lead to murder and destruction.

Murders: This is the act of the devil. It is the spirit that seeks to eliminate things. Wherever there is murder, the devil is the mastermind.

He is behind every wicked act that leads to murder. This includes such things as abortions, honor killings, human ritual sacrifices, killing of nations and what is good, wars, battles, medically assisted deaths, hatred, the list is endless. Jesus Christ called Satan a murderer from the beginning. The Bible also says anyone who is angry with his brother without a cause or hates his brother is a murderer. 1 John 3:15 says, "Whoever hastes his brother is a murderer and you know that no murderer has eternal life abiding in him." In Matthew 5:21-22 (NKJV), Jesus Christ says, "You have heard that it was said to those of old. 'You shall not murder, and whoever murders will be in danger of judgment.' But I say to you that whoever is angry with his brother without a cause shall be in danger of the judgment."

At the beginning of time, Cain, the first son of Adam, committed the first murder due to envy, anger and jealousy toward Abel, his brother. Cain was the child born after Adam and Eve committed a sin of disobedience against God, tempted by the devil to eat the fruit from the tree which God told them never to eat. They failed to resist the temptation. They ate and became spiritually dead and disconnected from God. Harkening to Satan caused humanity to fall from God's grace. This is how sin entered the earth. The bible says disobedience is a sin of witchcraft. So witchcraft was the first sin committed on earth.

Satan is the father of sin. He planted witchcraft to manipulate humanity. Determined to ensure sin is entrenched and crystalized on the earth, he entered into Cain who ended up killing Abel. Cain and Abel were both farmers. Cain farmed the land, and Abel farmed animals, was a shepherd. When the time to give an offering to the LORD God came, Abel brought a perfect offering, fat portions of the firstborn of his flock while Cain brought just any fruit of the ground as an offering. Abel's offering pleased the LORD God, while He had no regard for Cain's offering. This made Cain very angry, and it showed on his face. Before Cain committed murder, God spoke to him about his anger and advised him to do well next time and warned him of the sin encroaching at his door if he did not get rid of his anger.

God warned Cain about the sin that was coming to him. However, being a legalist, Satan took advantage of the anger in Cain and entered him to commit murder. Cain decided to deceive Abel into going out to the field with him, where he rose up and killed him. Later, when God asked Cain, "Where is your brother?" Cain said, "I don't know." Cain's attitude had Satan written all over it. His attitude was full of manipulation, deception, anger, envy, and jealousy which resulted in murder. The devil is the murderer from the beginning, as Jesus Christ noted in John 8:42-44.

No one can commit murder, lie and deceive without the help of the devil. Committing murder fulfills the plans and desires of the evil spirits.

In the story of Cain and Abel, we also learn about the blood of murdered human beings. It speaks against their murderers, and the earth that swallows the blood, curses the murderers and rejects them. We also learn that the earth has a mouth to swallow. Each time a person is murdered or an animal is killed, the earth opens her mouth to receive the blood. When Cain said to God, "I don't know," the LORD said, "What have you done? The voice of your brother's blood cries out to me from the ground. And now you are cursed from the earth, which has opened its mouth to receive your brother's blood from your hand. When you till the ground, it shall no longer yield its strength to you. A fugitive and a vagabond you shall be on the earth." Genesis 4:1-12 (NKJV).

This was a severe curse and reveals how serious, intense and grievous murder is in the spirit realms. In the physical, it might look like a quick and easy way to get rid of the unwanted people, such as an unwanted pregnancy. Today, to continue to ensure blood spills in great numbers on earth, as many societies got rid of death penalties, Satan tricked many societies to legalize abortion and protect this law with an iron fist.

Murder has been a pandemic on earth since the beginning of time to this day. The blood of human beings is very crucial in the spirit realms. Killing humans, who are made in the image and likeness of God, should give the enemy satisfaction for the personal vendetta he has against

God. The devils get the blood of human beings through various means, such as sickness, diseases, homicides, accidents of all kinds, killings with all sorts of weapons, spiritual murder using dark arts and hatred.

The good thing is that when Satan caused Judas, the Romans and the unbelieving Jews to kill Jesus Christ, he did not know that he was allowing the blood of God himself to spill on the earth to break the curse Adam allowed in the earth. Since the blood of murdered human beings speaks, the blood of Jesus Christ is always speaking in favor of born-again Christians and against their enemies and evil works of darkness. The blood of Jesus Christ cries to God on behalf of born-again Christians when they pray and cry to God. The blood of Jesus Christ gives born-again Christians victory over the enemy. It is important for born-again Christians to always invoke and plead the blood of Jesus Christ. Partaking in the Holy Communion is also critical.

The Bible also says murderers will not enter heaven, and will not inherit the kingdom of God. Knowing that Satan is the one who murdered first on earth and has no part in the kingdom of God in heaven, it makes sense and goes without saying that those who kill will be with Satan in hell. In Revelation 21:8 (KJV), it says, "But the fearful, and unbelieving, and the abominable, and the murderers, and the whoremongers, and the sorcerers, and idolaters, and all liars, shall have their part in the lake which burneth with fire and brimstone: which is the second death."

Drunkenness: This is a very destructive spirit. It breaks, and destroys lives, families and relationships. People can be drunk with alcohol, substances, blood, power or with sin. Drunkenness gives false comfort. Some people believe that they can drink their problems away, while others take refuge in sin to find comfort. This is a trap of the devil. People become addicted to alcohol, power and sin, believing and thinking it is the only way to live and sometimes, the only way out of challenges.

In Luke 21 (ESV) when Jesus Christ was telling about the future events, the wars, destruction of the Temple and Jerusalem, persecution, his second coming, he urged people to watch and pray saying in verse 34-36 that "But watch yourselves lest your hearts be weighed down with dissipation and drunkenness and cares of life, and that day come upon you suddenly like a trap. For it will come upon all who dwell on the face of the whole earth. But stay awake at all times, praying that you may have strength to escape all these things that are going to take place, and to stand before the Son of Man." Jesus Christ tells us that troubles will come upon the earth until he comes back, and the way to deal with them is to always pray and not to be hopeless, fall into a state of moral degradation, decay and drunkenness. The way to remain strong and overcome on earth is through prayer. Otherwise, drunkenness can become a solution to numbing the pain of the challenges of life.

Drunkenness is a sin, and an abomination linked to loudness, arguments, violence, sexual immorality, poverty and lack of wisdom. Proverbs 20:1 says, "Wine is a mocker, strong drink is a brawler, and whoever is led astray by it is not wise." Proverbs 23:20-21 says, "Do not be with heavy drinkers of wine or with gluttonous eaters of meat. For the heavy drinker and the glutton will come to poverty, and drowsiness will clothe one with rags." Isaiah 5:11 says, "Woe to those who rise early in the morning that they may pursue strong drink, who stay up late in the evening that wine may inflame them." Drunkenness brings curses in a person's life.

1 Corinthians 6:9-11 (KJV) says, "Know ye not that the unrighteous shall not inherit the kingdom of God? Be not deceived: neither fornicators, nor idolaters, nor adulterers, nor effeminates (sexual immorality/ prostitutes), nor abusers of themselves with mankind (homosexuals), nor thieves, nor covetous, nor drunkards, nor revilers (i.e. verbally abusive people, slander, foul language, coarse, harsh and bitter words), nor extortioners, shall inherit the kingdom of God. And such were some of you: but ye are washed, but ye are sanctified, but ye are justified in the name of the Lord Jesus, and by the Spirit of our God." Drunkenness cheats people of their dignity in life and eternity in the kingdom of God.

In the Bible, drunkenness does not only relate to wine and hard drinks. A person can be drunk with blood. In Isaiah 49:25 (NKJV) God says, "I will feed them that oppress you with their own flesh; and they shall be drunken with their own blood, as with sweet wine; and all flesh shall know that I the LORD am your Savior, and your redeemer, the Mighty one of Jacob." Killing believers for their testimony and witness of Jesus Christ is like the enemy being drunk with blood.

When God released judgments against the enemies in Deuteronomy 32:42 (NKJV), the expression of drunk with blood was used. It says, 'I will make my arrows drunk with blood, and my sword shall devour flesh, with the blood of the slain and the captives, from the heads of the leaders of the enemy."

A born-again Christian is urged to not be drunk with wine or anything, but to be filled with the Holy Spirit. It says in Ephesians 5:18 (ESV) that "And do not get drunk with wine, for that is debauchery, but be filled with the Spirit." This signifies that drunkenness is a spirit that is unholy, unclean and results in unholy, unclean outcomes. It is better to be filled with the Holy Spirit and deliver holy outcomes. The antidote against drunkenness is the fire of the Holy Spirit, active and alive in the believers of Jesus Christ.

Revelries: This refers to loud parties of all kinds. Living and loving a party life is driven by the spirit of revelries. Typically, such parties involve drunkenness, sexual immorality, debauchery and other abominable acts and behaviors associated with nightlife and nighttime. In Romans 13:13, it says, "Let us behave decently, as in the daytime, not in carousing and drunkenness (revelry), not in sexual immorality and debauchery, not in dissension and jealousy."

The party life is also associated with the behaviors and attitudes of unbelievers and carnality. Being born again does save people from the destructive party life. Cases of people who have been delivered from party lifestyle, and are now born again living a life directed by the Holy Spirit, are countless.

The abomination to God and Jesus Christ has escalated to another level at those parties. It is like there is a concerted effort to mock Christians and insult our Lord and Savior Jesus Christ. Some parades around the earth, like the 2019 and 2023 Brazilian parade, the 2024 Olympics games ceremonies in France and the 2022 Commonwealth Games opening ceremony in the UK, are just a few examples. The drive to venerate and exalt the powers of darkness is just part of Satan's attempts to fool people and discredit God in the eyes, hearts and minds of those that are lost.

The open, out-of-control indulgence in the acts of the flesh is pathetic. The actors, decision makers and approvers of those abominable acts are just puppets, agents of the devil, blinded to what matters, their eternity and life after their death. Everyone will stand before God and account for their actions here on earth.

Every soul that has ever lived on earth will face Jesus Christ for judgment. As for Satan and his minions, they are already judged. They know what is awaiting them at the end of time. They are working hard and tirelessly to recruit and fool people to implement their evil plans and trap many into eternity in hell, without God. The amazing thing is that there is always someone available to do the devil's bidding. Without Jesus Christ, no human being can overcome the tricks of the devil. This testifies that everyone needs salvation and a Savior. It is important to receive Christ as one's Lord and Savior to avoid falling into the trap of the enemy, which can last for generations in families and nations. This is where generational curses and blessings come.

Generational curses are because of people over generations refusing to accept the transformational and translational gift God gives through Jesus Christ. Refusing Jesus Christ and His gospel is rejecting God and his offer of salvation. Therefore, it makes it difficult to argue with the fact that people choose their afterlife destiny, heaven or hell. The earth is the only place where humanity makes a choice about their life after death.

Generational blessings are because of people who chose to obey God and accept His offer of salvation. The thing about generational curses and blessings is that, generations come and go, but what they have done, agreed to and accepted remains behind to rule in the next generations. It can be blessings or curses that rule in the lives of their descendants.

Choosing Jesus Christ reverses all the generational curses, and a new inheritance is established in the family and lineage that triggers the flow of generational blessings. Exodus 20:5-6; Deuteronomy 5:9-10; and Numbers 14:18-19 (NKJV) indicate that God is a God of generations.

In Exodus 20:5-6 and Deuteronomy 5:9-10 (NKJV), the Lord says, "You shall not bow to them (graven images/idols) nor serve them. For I, the LORD your God, am a jealous God, visiting the iniquity of the fathers upon the children to the third and fourth generations for those who hate me, but showing mercy to thousands, to those who love me and keep my commandments."

It says in Numbers 14:18-19 that "The LORD is longsuffering (slow to anger) and abundant in mercy, forgiving iniquity and transgression, but He by no means clears the guilty, visiting the iniquity of the fathers on the children to the third and fourth generation'. Pardon the iniquity of these people, I pray, according to the greatness of Your mercy, just as you have forgiven this people from Egypt even until now." Those who repent from the iniquities of their fathers, ask for forgiveness from God, can escape the judgement against those iniquities.

It is possible in any generation to turn the wheel of generational curses into generational blessings. In Ezekiel 18:20, it says, "The soul who sins shall die. The son shall not bear the guilt of the father, nor the father bear the guilt of the son. The righteousness of the righteous shall be upon himself, and the wickedness of the wicked shall be upon himself."

The Fruit of the Holy Spirit, which is Love, Peace, Joy, Patience, Kindness, Goodness, Faithfulness, Gentleness (Meekness) and Self-control, planted and rooted in a life lived in Christ, helps born-again

Christians to counter the acts and the lusts of the flesh. Without the Holy Spirit, the flesh rules and reigns in the lives of humanity, leading them away from God in this life and the life after.

GOD, THE CREATOR OF ALL HUMANS BUT THE FATHER OF SOME

It is important to note that God created all human beings, but not all human beings are His children. He created all humans in His likeness and image. He is the creator of all and not the Father of all. God gave all humans free will to choose Him as their Father or reject him and choose other spirits as their masters. Human beings are spirits clothed in mortal bodies. The human spirit, just like the human soul, lives forever. The human spirit belongs to God, and the human soul belongs to individual human beings. They can choose to make the Lord Jesus Christ the bishop and the shepherd of their souls or to allow Satan and his evil spirits to own their souls.

God is the Father only to those who believe in Jesus Christ as their Lord and Savior, the bishop and the Sheppard of their souls. Jesus Christ pointed this out quite clearly to the Jews who claimed to be the children of God yet hated him and rejected him and his teachings and words. In John 8:42-44 (NKJV), Jesus Christ said to them, "If God were your Father, you would love me, for I proceeded forth and came from God, nor have I come of Myself, but He sent me. Why do you not understand my speech? Because you are not able to listen to my word. You are of your father the devil, and the desires of your father you want to do. He was a murderer from the beginning, and does not stand in the truth, because there is no truth in him. When he speaks a lie, he speaks from his own resources (native language), for he is a liar and the father of it."

This implies that if a person is a child of God, they would hear and believe the words Jesus Christ speaks and would believe the gospel and be saved. The opposite is true. The others who are not the children of

God would refuse to hear the word of God, reject the gospel of Jesus Christ and the will of God, make themselves the children of the devil and therefore hear and do the will of the devil on earth. In John 8:44, Jesus Christ said to the Pharisees that "You are of your father the devil, and your will is to do your father's desires."

Unchecked, the heart can conceive evil that produces the acts of the flesh. The forces of darkness manipulate the heart, mind, thoughts and imagination as everything we do and say is birthed in the heart before it manifests in the physical. Without the help of the Holy Spirit, resisting the acts of the flesh can be close to impossible.

Every human being responds to a spirit; it can be the Spirit of God or the spirit of the enemy, the opposer. This is quite interesting. As humans, we all look the same, can be born in the same family in the physical, but are spiritually not the same and therefore born spiritually in different families. People can be related to one another physically but unrelated spiritually. People look the same physically, but spiritually different and divided. Therefore, those who are the children of God on earth would eventually be born of the Spirit of God and be translated from the kingdom of darkness ruled by the devil to the kingdom of God ruled by the Spirit of God.

The children of God are the heirs of salvation and the blessings of Abraham. However, since everyone is born in a fallen world, the heirs would remain subjected to the spirits of this world due to the original sin until their time of salvation comes. The heirs belong to Christ. In Galatians 3:29 and 4:1-8 (NKJV, NLT and NIV) Paul says, "And if you are Christ's, then you are Abraham's seed, and heirs according to promise. Now I say that the heir, as long as he is a child, does not differ at all from a slave, though he is master of all, but is under guardians and stewards until the time appointed by the father. And that's the way it was with us before Christ came. We were like children; we were slaves to the basic spiritual principles of this world. But when the right time came, God sent his Son, born of a woman, subject to the law. God sent him to buy freedom for us who were slaves to the law, so that he could adopt us as his very own children. And because we are his children,

God has sent the Spirit of his Son into our hearts, prompting us to call out, "Abba Father." Now you are no longer a slave but God's own child. And since you are his child, God has made you heir. Formerly, when you did not know God, you were slaves to so-called gods that do not even exist."

The heirs are redeemed by the blood of Jesus Christ from the hands of the gods of this world, Satan and his spiritual and physical minions. Jesus Christ, who is the master of the heirs of salvation, rules over all things and is the Father of all spirits. He rules over all that is in heaven, under the heaven and on earth. This includes even all unclean spirits such as Satan, fallen angels and demons and their agents on earth. This is the reason the unclean spirits, who could not fight Jesus back, begged him to not send them to the abyss where they belong, but rather allow them to go into the pigs, which when they entered them, they all went mad, ran into the river and drowned. In Matthew 28:18, Jesus Christ said, "All authority has been given to me in heaven and on earth." Jesus Christ is the first born of all the heirs of salvation.

The Bible also says in Philippians 2:9-10 (NKJV) that "Therefore God also has highly exalted Him and given Him the name which is above every name, that at the name of Jesus every knee should bow, of those in heaven, and of those on earth, and of those under the earth, and that every tongue should confess that Jesus Christ is Lord, to the glory of God the Father." This implies that those who are in Christ have been given power and authority over spirits that rule those who are without Jesus Christ.

The name of Jesus Christ and his gospel convict people. It separates the goats from the sheep. In Matthew 10:34-36 (NKJV), Jesus Christ said, "Do not think that I came to bring peace on earth. I did not come to bring peace but a sword. For I have come to 'set a man against his father, a daughter against her mother, and a daughter-in-law against her mother-in-law, and a man's enemies will be those of his own household." The sheep are those who are born-again by the Spirit of God and hear the voice of Jesus Christ and his word. The goats are those who reject salvation found only in Jesus Christ. Salvation in Christ is personal.

Those who receive salvation in Christ also receive the Holy Spirit. The Holy Spirit plants into the lives of believers, the Fruit of the Spirit that helps them navigate life in a fallen world and shields them from the princes of this earth.

ABOUT THE FRUIT OF THE HOLY SPIRIT:

The book of Galatians 5:22-23 also lists the Fruit of the Spirit, which are opposite to the acts of the flesh. The evidence of life ruled by the Fruit of the Spirit produces:

Love; Joy; Peace; Patience (Longsuffering); Gentleness; Goodness; Faith, Meekness (Humbleness); and Temperance (Self Control).

Both the lusts of the flesh and the Fruit of the Spirit cannot be touched. They are experiential and ruled by the spirit realms. However, there is a vast difference in the way the acts of the flesh and the Fruit of the Holy Spirit manifest on earth. The acts of the flesh are action-based while the Fruit of the Spirit is a state of being. People must take action to produce the lusts of the flesh. People choose their responses and attitudes toward circumstances to produce the Fruit of the Holy Spirit.

For most people, it is much easier to live life from the flesh than it is from the Fruit of the Spirit. A carnal life is basically the standard way of living for most people and societies due to the sin nature of the fallen world. Personal satisfaction lends itself perfectly to a fleshly life. Looking at the affections and lusts of the flesh against the Fruit of the Spirit, it is clear they are distinct and competing interests with two separate origins. The affections and the lusts of the flesh are from a dark place that destroys their perpetrators and sometimes for generations. Satan is the source of the affections and lusts of the flesh. Always ready to deceive with the intention to afflict at some point.

The Fruit of the Spirit originates from the Holy Spirit and reveals the nature of God and Jesus Christ. The Fruit of the Spirit flow from the transformed heart. When one walks under the check and conduct of the Fruit of the Spirit, it is not easy to engage in the affections and the lusts of the flesh. To be influenced by the Fruit of the Spirit requires paying conscious attention to one's heart, thoughts, words, and imagination. Filling the heart with the Word of God and prayer is vital to keeping a closer relationship with the Holy Spirit and the Fruit of the Spirit alive at every point.

Keeping the Word of God in the heart makes it easy for born-again Christians to meditate on the word of God, which in turn gives good success. The Holy Spirit helps born-again Christians to meditate on the word of God to keep the mind and heart grounded and bring success in their lives. A Christian meditation is not a state of mindlessness and quietness.

In Joshua 1:8, God reveals the path to lasting success. He instructed Joshua, saying, "This book of the law shall not depart from your mouth, but you shall meditate in it day and night, that you may observe to do according to all that is written in it. For then you will make your way prosperous, and then you will have good success."

A Christian meditation is proclaiming the Word of God in our hearts, singing hymns and psalms. In Ephesians 5:18, it says, "Do not get drunk with wine, which leads to debauchery. Instead, be filled with the Spirit, speaking to one another with psalms, hymns, and songs from the Spirit. Sing and make music from your heart to the Lord, always giving thanks to God the Father for everything, in the name of our Lord Jesus Christ."

In Psalm1:1-2 (NKJV), it says, "Blessed is the man who walks not in the counsel of the ungodly, nor stands in the path of sinners, nor sits in the seat of the scornful; but his delight is in the law of the LORD, and in his law, he meditates day and night."

Christian meditation is more like an inaudible prayer as they go through the day, known only to the meditator and God. It takes practice and regular reading of the Bible as revealed by the Holy Spirit to build up an attitude of Christian meditation. Also, the Holy Spirit is the one who prints the Word of God in the hearts of born-again believers and the greatest helper when engaging in Christian meditation. He is the one who gives all the understanding and brings into remembrance the Word of God when meditating. Without the Holy Spirit, there is no power in a Christian. Also, a prayerless Christian is a powerless Christian. The Holy Spirit is the one who helps Christians to pray.

Anyone who proclaims Jesus Christ as their Lord and Savior but does not keep their light burning by the power of the Holy Spirit is just like a car driving a long distance without enough gas to reach the destination, with no hope of ever reaching the destination. Our destination is heaven reserved only for those who worship God in truth and in Spirit. Without the Holy Spirit, it is much challenging and difficult for a Christian to be a Christian. Compromises and lukewarmness can easily become the norm and a standard difficult to mend. An empty Christian is typically prone to mistakes, gullible to the acts of the flesh and the influence of Satan, demons and evil agents of darkness much easily, committing habitual sins that can become iniquities for themselves and their descendants. It is possible to call oneself a Christian but still build a foundation fertile for generational curses. An empty Christian is a religious Christian who compromises, is neither born again nor filled with the Holy Spirit. To be filled with the Holy Spirit, born-again believers can ask for Him from God, or hands can be laid upon them to receive the baptism of the Holy Spirit. There are a lot of religious Christians.

Jesus Christ never calls anyone to go into the world without empowering them with the power of the Holy Spirit. The baptism of the Holy Spirit and Fire is critical to a successful Christian life. In the book of Acts, Jesus Christ commanded the disciples to wait for the Helper before they went out into the world to preach the good news to all creatures, with signs and wonders following. It says in Acts 1:4

(NKJV) that "And being assembled together with them, He commanded them not to depart from Jerusalem, but to wait for what the Father had promised "which" he said "you heard of from me, for John truly baptized with water, but you shall be baptized with the Holy Spirit not many days from now."

He said he was going to ask the Father to send the Holy Spirit to come and help, comfort and advocate for the disciples, the Christians. The Holy Spirit is a gift reserved only for the true believers in Christ Jesus who are saved by grace through faith in the finished work of the cross of Calvary.

The Holy Spirit, Salvation and Spiritual Deliverance

It is true that it is only by the grace of God that people are saved. For people to receive that grace, it is the work of the Holy Spirit and not anyone's own efforts. Mental and physical abilities and strength are not required for salvation. Salvation is the biggest miracle that anyone can ever receive. It is the perfect work of the Holy Spirit. It does not require intellect. If one looks at salvation from an intellectual perspective, one will never be saved. To be saved, we believe by faith and confess that Jesus Christ is the Son of God, who came to redeem us by his shed blood at the cross of Calvary, reconciled us to God and made us children of God.

A Christian's salvation and redemption were purchased at a huge price, involving the birth, the death and the resurrection of Jesus Christ. This is not to be taken for granted. It is the most precious gift that separates the sheep from the goats.

You literally become a member of God's family. God's family is big on earth and in heaven. God becomes your Father, He never dies, is always there and gives heavenly blessings to His children. What makes a human being a child of God is believing in His Son, Jesus Christ and taking Him as one's Lord and Savior. Those who reject salvation through Jesus Christ alone are not the children of God.

A truly saved person walks in the power of the Holy Spirit and is always under the check and control of the Spirit of God. So, I believe grace without the Holy Spirit cannot be sustained. Once saved, a believer needs to pray for Jesus Christ to baptize them with the Holy Spirit to be able to live a saved, Christian life. As John the Baptist said, "I baptize you with water, but he who is mightier than I is coming, the thong of whose sandals I am not worthy to untie, he will baptize you with the Holy Spirit and with fire" Luke 3:16.

A true Christian is baptized by a human being in the name of the Father, the Son and the Holy Spirit by immersion in the water and immediately receives the Holy Spirit to live in them. This does not mean they have a relationship with the Holy Spirit. However, Jesus Christ himself baptizes with the Holy Spirit and Fire. There is a difference between just having the Holy Spirit abiding in a believer and those who have been baptized in the Holy Spirit.

The goal of a born-again Christian should be to ask Jesus Christ for the baptism of the Holy Spirit. No man can do this for anyone, no matter how anointed they are. Only Jesus Christ does this. A person who is already baptized in the Holy Spirit can lay their hands on believers and pray to the Father to baptize them with the Holy Spirit, and Jesus Christ will do it. A person who desires to be baptized in the Holy Spirit can also pray to the Father, and they can receive the baptism. It is important to ask God for the Holy Spirit.

Jesus Christ said that "When we ask for the Holy Spirit, God will not give us anything else that is not the Holy Spirit. In Matthew 7:11 Jesus Christ says, "If you then being evil, know how to give good gifts to your children, how much more will your Father who is in heaven give good gifts to those who ask Him." In Luke 11:13, it says, "If you then, being evil, know how to give good gifts to your children, how much more will your heavenly Father give the Holy Spirit to those who ask Him."

I once prayed in tongues before I went to bed. When I was sleeping, I dreamed of three men in suits, the middle one dressed in a blue suit and the others on the left and right wore black suits. They were coming into my bedroom. The one in the middle said to me, "You have to stop." I understood that the evil being meant I must stop praying in tongues. I said, "Who are you?" and he said he was Satan. I suddenly saw a long blue whip in my right hand, and I whipped it and chased them away, calling on the name of Jesus Christ, and they left running for their lives. Like the Bible says in Deuteronomy 28:7 (NKJV) that "The LORD will cause your enemies who rise against you to be defeated before your face, they shall come out against you one way and flee before you seven ways."

As Jesus Christ said in the Lord's Prayer, "Thy will be done on earth as it is in heaven, give us this day our daily bread." God gives his children the Holy Spirit, His Spirit to live in and with His children, so they can do the will of God and overcome the tricks of the enemy daily. This is nothing like a physical and biological father can ever give. God gives far more than we even deserve, which is called grace. You come to receive and enjoy the companionship of the Holy Spirit through grace. The Holy Spirit brings deliverance in the lives of born-again believers.

When the Holy Spirit comes into a person, the evil spirits that were there before are dealt with very powerfully and effectively. The Holy Spirit launches a spiritual warfare against evil spirits that had sought homage in the person before coming to Christ. Expect a spiritual and sometimes physical battle once a person becomes a born-again believer. Crossing the floor from darkness into the light, one should expect a spiritual battle to ensue. Darkness will fight, wanting to hold on to what does not and have never really belonged to it. Darkness hijacks people, and once they are captured, they never want to let go.

Thankfully, once a person becomes God's child, darkness loses power over the person as they go through deliverance and must give way. The person also receives more powerful support and help than all the forces of darkness combined. Deliverance can be a process. It can take days, months or years. This process can take a short or long period. This was my case. I believe the Lord allows the deliverance process to take its course so we can fully understand where we come from spiritually, the depth of the dark places we have been, so we can appreciate and embrace our salvation, deliverance and the light he gives us.

There is a misconception that once a person is born again, they do not need spiritual deliverance that commands evil spirits to leave the host and the oppressed. In my experience, once a person proclaims Jesus Christ as their Lord and Savior, unimaginable spiritual warfare begins. This can compel born-again believers to seek deliverance not only by reading the Bible and praying, but also by casting out evil spirits in the name of Jesus Christ, or they can die prematurely as forces of darkness go on a rampage against them.

The process of deliverance can be very painful, as it was in my case. The road to deliverance can be very challenging and can never be travelled solo. That is why the Bible in Hebrews 10:25 says "Never forsake the gathering of the saints."

Embarking on the pilgrimage from Egypt to Israel, following the route the children of Israel took when they left Egypt to go to the Promised Land in Israel, gave me a clear perspective of what it takes to be delivered from the hands of the oppressors.

You truly need Jesus Christ, the Holy Spirit and heavenly holy hosts nearby all the time to be fully and completely delivered from the hands of the enemy. The good thing is that God gives born-again believers the weapons to fight with. He also provides those he has anointed to help in the journey to complete spiritual deliverance. The Bible says in 2 Corinthians 10:4 (NKJV) that "For the weapons of our warfare are not carnal, but mighty in God for the pulling down of strongholds."

The oppressors of humanity are evil powers, forces of darkness, their evil human agents and strongholds in a person's life. They do not let go without a fight. You need faith and endurance that can only be found in the Holy Spirit. It also helps to have spiritual support from those anointed to demonstrate the power of the name of Jesus Christ and the Holy Spirit. Through the deliverance process, I have learned that the prayers of Christians are not equal. Some prayers break the yokes, while some prayers provoke demons and the powers of darkness. Christians do not have the same anointing. Some are more anointed than the others.

These days, technology helps Christians to be strong, have more faith and learn from one another in person and virtually. In the spirit realm, there is no distance. Time and space do not exist in the spirit realm. Christians from any part of the world can participate in a service hosted from a far-flung country and still receive by faith their healing, deliverance and blessings released from that pulpit. A Christian lives by faith. However, virtual deliverance pales in comparison to in-person deliverance. There are issues that can be delivered from a distance, by self-deliverance, fasting, prayer and reading the Bible. However, deeper spiritual issues need a different kind of deliverance and the higher anointing, calling on the name of Jesus Christ. Not everyone claiming to be a deliverance minister has the required higher anointing. The Holy Spirit directs believers to the anointing they need to deal with their unique issues and conditions.